GROWING UP
A SULLEN BAPTIST
AND OTHER LIES

Robert Flynn

University of North Texas Press
Denton, Texas

Collection Copyright © 2001 Robert L. Flynn

A Baptist Looks Askance, City of Fire, The Combined Platoon, Understanding Vietnam, India-the Divided Crowd, Copyright 2001, Robert Flynn

Foreword by Joyce Gibson Roach, copyright 2001, University of North Texas Press

All Rights Reserved
Printed in the United States of America
First Edition

6 5 4 3 2 1

The paper in this book meets the minimum requirements of the American National Standard for Permanence of Paper for Printed Library Materials, Z39.48.1984

Permissions:
University of North Texas Press
PO Box 311336
Denton, TX 76203-1336
940-565-2142

Library of Congress
Cataloging-in-Publication Data
Flynn, Robert, 1932–
   Growing up a sullen Baptist and other lies / by Robert Flynn.--1st ed.
   p. cm.
   ISBN 1-57441-127-6 (alk. paper)
   1. Flynn, Robert, 1932– .
   2. Novelists, American--20th century--Biography. 3. Baptists--United States--Biography. I. Title.

PS3556.L9 G7 2001
813'.54--dc21   2001027962

Cover Artwork by Deirdre Flynn Bass
Design by Angela Schmitt

Permissions:
   Growing Up a Sullen Baptist copyright 1999, Robert Flynn. First appeared in a slightly different version in The Door Magazine, January/February, March/April, May/June, 1999.
   Miracles in Chillicothe copyright 2000, Robert Flynn. First appeared in a slightly different version in The Door Magazine, May / June, July/August, September/October, November/December, 2000.
   A Sense of Place copyright 1990, Texas Folklore Society, reprinted by permission. First appeared in F.E. Abernethy, ed., The Bounty of Texas, University of North Texas Press, 1990.
   Enduring Love copyright 2000, Robert Flynn. First appeared in the Dallas Morning News, February 13, 2000, as "40th Anniversary Trip Didn't Make Them Want to Pack It In."
   Lions in Camp copyright 1998, Robert Flynn. First appeared in a slightly different version in Deborah Douglas, ed., Stirring Prose, Texas A&M University Press, 1998.
   Truth and Beauty copyright 1986, Robert Flynn. First appeared in a slightly different version in Texas Journal of Ideas, History and Culture, Texas Council for the Humanities, Fall/Winter 1996. Reprinted by permission.
   Jeremiah was a Bulldog copyright 1997, Robert Flynn. First appeared in a slightly different version in David Rosenberg, ed., Communion, Anchor Books/Doubleday, 1997.
   Hooked on Heroes copyright 1991, Robert Flynn. First appeared in a slightly different version in San Antonio Light, January 28, 1991.
   Still the Street Without Joy copyright 1991, Robert Flynn. First appeared in a slightly different version in Kali Tal, ed., The Viet Nam Generation, Vol. 3, Number 3, November 1991, The Viet Nam Generation, Inc., and Burning Cities Press 1991.
   Understanding Pol Pot and Pot Pol Legacy copyright 1989, Robert Flynn. First appeared in a slightly different version in The San Antonio Express-News, September, 1989, reprinted by permission.
   John Wayne Must Die copyright 1994, Robert Flynn. First appeared in a slightly different version in Kali Tal, ed., The Viet Nam Generation, Big Book, Vol. 6, The Viet Nam Generation, Inc. and Burning Cities Press 1994.

To Joe Bass

Other books by Robert Flynn:

North to Yesterday

In the House of the Lord

The Sounds of Rescue, the Signs of Hope

Season Rain, and other stories

When I was Just Your Age, with Susan Russell
(published by UNT Press)

A Personal War in Vietnam

Wanderer Springs

The Last Klick

Living with the Hyenas

The Devils Tiger, with Dan Klepper

Tie-Fast Country

Table of Contents

Foreword

—

"Just A Plain Country Boy"

Bob Flynn needs no introduction, but he does need explaining. Robert Lopez Flynn came into the world on April 12, 1932. He was born and grew up in Chillicothe, Texas, on a farm that has been in the family for over 100 years. The place might be labeled "mighty plain," typical of scores of rural, hard-scrabble locations in West Texas. Such farming communities exist in east Texas, too, but trees, woods, even forests offer opportunities for little towns to be pretty, soft, even charming. But, "plain" is just the right description of Chillicothe - treeless, unadorned, level, ordinary, unrefined, without pretensions, strung out between rows of something on the High Plains - cotton, grain, Chillicothe, cotton, grain. Oh, and windy, hot and waterless; or windy, cold and icy. Bob recalls, "I am a native of Chillicothe by intention. I intended to be born there and I intended to live there the rest of my life. You know what happens to good intentions." His sojourn in Chillicothe was filled with plain events, such as his life as a hoer - excuse me, hoe handler - in the cotton fields and other mundane tasks on the farm and in town. The only deviation from the pattern was when the farm boy joined the Marines during the Korean War.

Bob jumps from the frying pan into the fire by proclaiming loudly the second flaw in his life. He's a Baptist: "I didn't intend to be a Baptist. Well, I intended to be one when I was young and needed someone to tell me I was better than anyone else, but I had hoped that by the time I had reached this stage of life that fact would be self-evident and I could become a fun-loving Methodist." Not only did he not become a Methodist, he grew into a sullen Baptist.

Both plain place and plain religion shaped the life of the country boy. Jean entered Bob's life in 1952, just after he returned from military service, and rescued him, even if he didn't know he needed saving beyond total immersion. They were married in 1953 and went to Baylor in Waco where Bob graduated in 1954. After attending Southwestern Baptist Seminary in Fort Worth for a year, he returned to Baylor in 1955 to earn a Masters in Speech and Drama. In 1957 the couple moved to North Carolina. Here, Bob taught at Gardner Webb Baptist Junior College, and their daughters were born, Deirdre in 1958 and Brigid in 1959. The family returned to Baylor where Bob taught. Jean had her degree by then and taught at University High School in Waco for a year. In the Fall of 1962, the entire drama department at Baylor resigned over censorship of "Long Days Journey Into Night." Trinity University in San Antonio hired the full department in 1963 and the family lived, as Jean says, "an idyllic life" until Brigid's death in 1971. Deirdre graduated from high school in 1976 and Jean finished the Master of Library Science degree that same spring, and began to write, too, focusing on biographies of famous Texas heroes and heroines. In the last few years Jean occasionally takes Bob on in readings, trying to tell the truth about certain matters in their lives which he insists on disremembering.

Except for Bob's service in the Marines, he undertook only one other experience without Jean and that was in 1970 when he spent two months in Vietnam as a war correspondent.

I first heard Robert Flynn in 1974 when he spoke at a Texas Folklore Society meeting in Abilene, Texas. He read a short story, "The Great Plain.", which offers a stark narrative about a couple, Grover and Edna Turrill. The piece is discussed here, in *Truth and Beauty*. I can remember thinking that if Bob Flynn never wrote another word, it would be enough. In a brief story, he captured in lean, sparse prose, clean-cutting as a plow trenching a furrow, the vagaries of land, weather, the human condition and the endurance of the human spirit against terrible odds.

Bob, of course, has written more words, many more, since "The Great Plain." In 1999 the Texas Institute of Letters, of which Bob has been president, bestowed on him the Lon Tinkle Award for Lifetime Achievement in recognition of his award-winning life in words - fiction and non-fiction books, stories, articles, personal narratives, essays, and speeches - which he continues to write.

The same writing style employing clean, sparse, plain syntax and language that occurs in "The Great Plain" may also be said to characterize much of Flynn's works. It remains only to point out that Flynn's humor, his particular brand of funny, does not occur in "The Great Plain" but appears in almost every other piece of his writing. If the qualities of style ground his writing, it is his humor that greases the wheels, lubricating his prose in ways that startle, surprise and make the reader laugh - howl is more like it - usually at the human condition. Like rain in West Texas, the humor comes when needed most, sometimes unexpectedly.

Most important, Bob is a great story-teller, able to draw the reader into his world, narrow as a cotton row, but recognizable in any country, any culture, any period in time. The heart and success of most of his writing celebrates the ordinary, simple, backward, clumsy, laughable, decent, un-heroic men and women of West Texas who resemble "folks" everywhere.

The various pieces in this volume prove that Robert Flynn is just a country boy, a plain man who is plain spoken, just plain funny. He is the plain-song of the plain town - the simple melody with no harmonies, a one line tune with no accompaniment. Before I get too carried away with the musical image, I need to remind myself that Robert Flynn can't carry a tune in a bucket.

Yes, he is just a plain, country boy - a man at home in the world, or the universe.

Joyce Gibson Roach

Introduction ⟶

I didn't have an ideal youth but it may be fair to say I had an idealistic youth. The center of my life was family, church, school, country in roughly that order. My home was full of love and also strife. My church was full of faith and also prejudice. The school I attended had diversity and segregation. My country exhibited oneness during World War Two but behind the show was a class war, a race war, a political war, even war between the branches of military service. The media was one propaganda arm of the government and the church was another.

I was unaware of much of that; the rest I overlooked. I overlooked it in order to believe that my family was indivisible, that if the whole world were Christian, especially if they were Baptist Christians, the world would be full of love and peace. I believed that those of us who were able to finish high school and go to college were morally and intellectually superior. I believed that we were one nation, under God, one people united by goodness against the forces of evil. I believed in a Good War and that killing Japanese and Germans for a good cause was a good thing.

I carried that veil of ignorance into the Marines believing it was my patriotic and religious duty to go to Korea and kill someone. It was not a duty that I thought distasteful. I rather looked forward to carrying God's name onto the battlefield and destroying evil, or at least the human face of evil.

I prayed that I would be sent to Korea almost as much as I prayed for anything in my life. How could God not let me be a hero? I believed my prayers had been answered when I was assigned to a replacement draft. A few days before the draft shipped out for Korea, I was reassigned to the rifle range to assist others on their way to Korea to hit the bullseye.

The Marines showed me a world truer than the one my church, my family, the schools I attended, or the newspapers, magazines and books I read had shown me. I struggled to understand a world my training, as a Baptist and as a Marine, did not equip me to control, to improve, or to escape.

I found it hard to reconcile Jesus who said his followers would be recognized by their love and my Drill Instructor who said a Marine was a professional killer and proud of it. I was very late in discovering what talk radio and televangelists found first—that peace is harder to achieve than war and that anger, hate and prejudice are less work than love. I also discovered that people are lazy and easily drift into anger, hatred, prejudice and war. Especially when goaded by talk radio hosts and televangelists who know what every Marine knows, its easier to attack a pillbox or a politician than to love your neighbor, much less your enemy. Someone said a cynic is a disappointed idealist. I think disappointed idealist is redundant.

I tried to slip back into the comfortable church world that pretended all men were brothers made in the image of God, that those who claimed Christ's name were guided by love in business, politics, church, and personal relationships; that greed, ambition and love of power were less evident in Christians than in other believers or non-believers. That America was God's favorite country.

That voluntary veil of ignorance wasn't rent in twain from the top to the bottom. It was abraded so slowly as to be almost imperceptible. Some of it was learning that many Americans profited from the misery, grief, death and destruction of World War Two, that some US merchants aided our enemies. That taxpayers had to pay an American company for the German ball-bearing plant at Schweinfurt bombed at great cost by US airmen. And for every palm tree destroyed or damaged in fighting on Guadalcanal.

Some of the veil parted when I met Germans and Japanese who prayed to the same God I did, and loved their country as much as I loved mine. Some of the veil was slashed when I learned that the destruction of German and Japanese imperialists empowered Stalin and Mao who each sponsored a holocaust that killed more people than Hitler. Some of it was shredded by people, even Christians, who called World War Two "The Good War" because we emerged victorious, self-righteous, and the most powerful nation in the world. As though a war, or a disease, or a natural disaster could ever be good. A war may be necessary but it cannot be good.

Some of the veil was frayed by classmates who found college life too blissful, their personal ambition too important to be bothered by the interests of the United States, or the United Nations, or the people of Korea. Who cared?

Much of the veil was fretted by Vietnam. Not the war itself, because it did, after all, mark the end of Communist expansion and the beginning of the Soviet implosion. Not because of opposition to the war because no war should be unopposed or without controversy. But much of the opposition to the war was empty sloganeering, heated rhetoric, selfish profiteering by the privileged who mimicked the rags of the poor and the uniforms of those who were not exempt from duty to their country.

Part of it was tattered by students who whined that they had been born into a terrible time. These were children of parents who had grown up during the Depression and fought a World War. They were children of privilege who had never had to work and would never have to serve their country. Their parents had given them everything but a sense of responsibility.

Any of the threadbare veil left was rent when my youngest daughter died. It was no one's fault and there was nothing I could do to prevent it. That was not the world for which I had been educated or trained. It was not the world that I had found in books and art, although that world was present in libraries and museums. I had looked on the wrong shelves. That world was even present in the Bible but I had preferred the verses that spoke of rest instead of work, peace rather than war, joy rather than sorrow.

There is no greater human tragedy than the death of a child, yet I did not want to be the kind of person who was exempt from the possibility of such a tragedy, immune to fevers, boils and poverty. An edenic Adam incapable of the heights or depths of Job.

I have tried to re-train for Job's world and through words and stories to update the survival kit I had been given as a youth. Mostly I have grappled with Job's world vicariously through characters I have invented, but fiction is slow and indirect and focused on concept more than idea. Sometimes I have wanted to address that world more quickly and directly and have written essays, a few over a number of years.

Pontius Pilate wasn't the first to ask, "What is truth?" Nor the last. Whatever truth is, it isn't nonfiction. These are opinions based on the information that I have, informed by my experience and by my faith. But the world is too complex for any writer or painter, philosopher, physicist or theologian. The very best capture but a moment or give us but a glimpse. The world is far too complex for any one genre, any one voice.

I have found it impossible to live far from the roots of the tree from whence I fell. I choose to live in Texas and believe if you live most of your life in the same place you better know what it looks like to other people. I travel less to discover other places than to discover the place of my birth. Nevertheless, other places are fascinating and it is easy to see them as symbols of larger concerns.

Jerusalem is an almost perfect example of religious strife with Christians, Muslims and Jews trying to gain control of their "holy" sites. As though any place were more sacred than another, or that any piece of ground could be more sacred than love.

India is another example of religious strife. Islam, Hinduism, Christian, Sikh, all strive to control their own destiny, and therefore, the portion of others. In addition, India's caste system adds to the burden of many and slows that country's rise to economic power.

The Khmer Rouge were a near perfect example of fundamentalism gone to seed. Pol Pot had teachers, professionals, and priests put to death or pulling plows. Cities were deserted in an attempt to recreate a literal Garden of Eden on top of the killing fields.

In nonfiction, as in fiction, the point does not have to be readily apparent. There are times when a writer wants the reader to draw the conclusion even when the reader may be unwilling to do so. In nonfiction, as in fiction, the opinion expressed may not be that of the writer but of a character or persona. And in nonfiction, as in fiction, the voice is crucial whether that voice be conversational, scholarly, pedantic, ironic, humorous, satirical, sarcastic or angry.

I have tried to find the correct voice for honest reasons knowing that some of those voices are dangerous. Humor may be taken lightly, satire may be misunderstood, sarcasm and anger may be offensive, even to those who are in agreement. Almost three centuries later, *Gulliver's Travels* and "A Modest Proposal" are still misunderstood by some and offensive to others.

And none of these voices, opinions, views are for everyone, for any time, or forever.

Baptist

Growing Up a Sullen Baptist ⟶

I am a sullen Baptist. In Chillicothe, a sullen Baptist was what you were if you couldn't get into the Methodist Church.

For those of you who may have never encountered a Baptist, I will attempt a definition.

If Christianity is the bread of life, Baptists are the crust.

If Christianity is the wine of life, Baptists are grape juice. You didn't get high but you don't get hiccups, either.

If Christianity covers the world like Sherwin Williams, Baptists cover Texas like a wet blanket.

Christianity has not conquered the world, but Baptists have surrounded Waco.

Baptists believe it is a sin to think evil of anyone. However, we do not believe it is a mistake. Baptists live lives of quiet vituperation.

Baptists believe the errors in the Bible were put there by God.

Baptists have fine-tuned right and wrong. As a Baptist, you can do almost anything as long as you don't enjoy it, drink it in public, do it to music, or continue it after ten p.m. Baptists still equate goodness with going to bed early. That's why they live so long. A Baptist will outlive a high-life Methodist every time.

Perhaps I should explain to you that there are different kinds of Baptists in case you think they are alike. Baptists don't really believe John the Baptist started the Baptist Church. If there is a biblical reference to Baptists, perhaps it is the New Testament reference to divers diseases. The most obvious feature of Baptists is their diversity. There are more than thirty distinct Baptist organizations in this country alone. Where you have two Baptists, you have a Baptist church. Where you have three Baptists you have two Baptist churches.

A moderate Baptist believes all Baptists have souls.

A conservative Baptist believes only Conservative Baptists have souls.

A liberal Baptist believes even Methodists have souls.

In Chillicothe we were liberal Baptists. We believed that Methodists had souls. It was a conscience they were lacking. I went to the Methodist Church once. The sons of bitches were singing our songs.

I never forgave them for that. For revenge I dated a Methodist girl. In Chillicothe we used to say, go with a Baptist get a freeze, go with a Methodist get a squeeze.

Every time I dated Myrna Dean, I had to talk to her mother about theology. Her mother always met me on the porch and her big old Doberman named Adolph came with her. I tried to explain to her the eternal security of the believer while Adolph demonstrated a romantic attachment to my leg.

"Methodists believe people can back-slide," Myrna Dean's mother said. "Baptists believe that once you're baptized you can do anything you want to," she said. "Be as wicked as you please."

In spite of Adolph, I listened because she was Myrna Dean's mother and because if I ever found out where that church was, I was going to run away from home and join it.

I never did find that church but Myrna Dean found a new boyfriend. Ray Dean Tooley. He was a fire bug. Myrna Dean went to a lot of barbecues but she never married because the church burned down. The church smoldered for weeks and was once mistaken for a diesel truck.

That couldn't happen to a Baptist Church. Baptists went in for Neo-penal architecture. When we learned about the Bastille in school we knew exactly what it looked like. We had gone to church in one.

Myrna Dean broke up with Roy Dean because he was always trying to light her cigarette and she didn't smoke. She was the only girl in my graduating class who had no bangs. No eyelashes. No eye brows. And butter on her nose.

I hope I haven't made Baptist life seem grim. We had our excitements, besides watching the Methodists go to hell. We had grave cleaning day. We all went to the cemetery and pulled weeds.

At grave cleaning you could put cockleburs in a girl's hair and drop red ants down her back. If you loved her. If you were just trifling you were restricted to grasshoppers and grassburrs.

One year I put a red ant down Norma Jean's dress, put cockleburs in her hair, and grassburrs in her shoes. I was a romantic fool.

When we had grave cleaning, we cleaned all the graves, even the Methodist graves. You could always tell a Methodist grave. They had more decorations on their tombstones than we had on our church.

They wrote sentimental messages on them. "Rest in peace." "Sacred to the memory of." We didn't put things like that on our tombstones. We knew that if a person had been a good Baptist, he was glad to go. We put cheerful things on our tombstones. "Free at last." Or, "T.G.I.F." Thank God it's final.

The reason we cleaned all the graves, even the Methodist graves, was because if we didn't, the weeds would get so high somebody could sneak in and make love on grandpa's grave. Nothing made a Baptist madder than someone making love over his dead body.

We had after-school activities. It was called Conformation Club. If you didn't conform, they hit you with the club. We had a club room with sayings on the wall. "Thou shalt not go with girls who shave their legs." Smooth legs were sure signs of a Methodist temptress. If God had wanted girls to have hairless legs he would have given them legs like chickens. God did give some of them legs like chickens. However, most Baptist girls had legs like gorillas.

"Thou shalt be in bed by ten p.m." A Baptist is smart enough to know that at 10 o'clock a boy is going to start thinking about going to bed. And the faster you get him there, the smaller his chances are of taking someone with him. If Baptists were allowed to stay up until midnight, there would be more Baptists than Catholics.

The Conformation Club had an illustrated Bible. With the pictures of Adam and Eve removed. Bathsheba bathed while wearing a robe. The seraphims had their cherubims covered.

The illustrated Bible gave us a distorted notion of human nature. Also human anatomy. I was a fifteen-year-old boy, wearing my best Levis, the shirt my mother had to iron twice to get the crease right, smelling of dad's shaving lotion although he wouldn't trust me with his razor, sitting in a Chevy pickup with a knob on the steering wheel for fast maneuvering.

Beside me was a fifteen-year-old girl wearing her sister's blouse, her mother's perfume, and her father's socks—stuffed in her brasserie. I looked at those soft, yielding eyes, those smooth pouty lips, those wooly boobs. And I knew why Methodists didn't believe in immersion. No one likes the smell of wet wool.

The only thing missing from the Conformation Club reading room was books. Baptists don't go in much for books, and ideas, and things like that. Show me a man who gets to reading and thinking about things and I'll show you a Methodist. Reading and thinking will change a fellow. Haskell Quinby got to reading one day and discovered he was a Virgo. Well, that scared the heck out of the rest of us.

While we didn't go in for ideas, we were keen on attitudes. We could take up an attitude quicker than an Episcopalian could take a drink. We had attitudes for everything. We had a Sunday attitude that said, I am bound for the promised land. And a Friday night attitude that said, you are bound for hell. And an election day attitude that said, God is a Republican. And Jesse Helms is his prophet.

For socializing we had Sunday School. The reason men went to Sunday School was to get away from their wives. They wouldn't let husbands and wives sit together in Sunday School. It had something to do with Numbers. Or Deuteronomy.

Orville Scott had perfect attendance for twenty years. Orville's wife, Myrna, was a clacker. Whenever he did something she didn't like, Myrna clacked her false teeth. Some days their house sounded like fifty castanets at a Mexican fandango. Myrna could go through a set of false teeth in three years. She wore out two dish towels giving him the silent treatment.

When Orville died Myrna clacked all the way through the funeral service. She sat beside her mother who wore a neck brace and couldn't throw up. It was the worse funeral Chillicothe ever had. More people were satisfied with the Republican primary.

We had baptism, which could be real exciting because the baptistery was always cold and damp. Bubba Dismuke used to keep his tadpoles in ours. Just when he had a good crop started, old man Sealy was born again and had to be baptized. Bubba couldn't take all the tadpoles home so he turned off the hot water heater so it wouldn't scald his toads.

That night a norther blew in and by morning it was near freezing. The pastor slipped a robe over his boxer shorts and stepped into the baptistery. "God almighty," he prayed. "Thank you for the adversity you send to make us strong."

Old man Sealy was not as thankful for adversity. When his bare foot hit the cold water he tried to back out. Too late. The pastor had a death grip and he was determined not to experience the Lord's adversity alone.

The pastor was getting the best of Sealy but the old man was fighting. The cold water came up over Sealy's knees, and over his thighs, and when it hit his private parts, old and arthritic as he was, Sealy leapt out of the water and using the pastor's arm for a pivot, made two laps around the baptistery before he went under again. The next time he surfaced he made it through the choir and all the way out of the church. That was the day it rained tadpoles in the choir loft. The pastor tried to dismiss the congregation but his teeth chattered so some people thought Myrna Scott had risen from the dead. It was a day of miracles in Chillicothe.

For entertainment we had prayer meetings. Our best prayer meetings were for rain. We had a lot of prayers for rain. Brother Maynard was the best pray-er we ever had. I still remember one of his prayers. "Lord, we need rain. It's awful dry down here. And, Lord, you haven't done anything for us since lightning struck the Methodist Church."

For community involvement we had missions. Young people were supposed to have a mission. I don't know why it was restricted to young people but it was. Bubba Spivey got to thinking about a mission and one day he announced he was going to be a missionary to the nudists. There weren't a lot of nudists who were Baptists. "Think what they save on choir robes," Bubba said. It takes a powerful lot of faith to be a Baptist but you can get by on very little logic.

Bubba had a hard time selling the church on his mission to the nudists. Most folks thought if God had wanted people to go naked he wouldn't have given them so much to hide. Besides, women folks didn't like the way Bubba looked at them when he said, "I don't see enough of you in church."

We had revivals. A revival had the excitement of a football game, the noise level of a rock concert, the emotional intensity of a high school romance in its third week, and the intellectual content of a fraternity initiation. Not many churches could stand more than one or two a year.

During revivals we had pack the pew night. Everybody was supposed to go out and goad others into coming so that each of us could pack a pew. I always invited Elvira Perkins. Elvira Perkins was so big she could pack a pew by herself and still have a hip in the aisle.

Elvira had buried three husbands and a hunting dog. Her last husband was run over by a train. The dog was run over by a bus. It was a Greyhound bus. That's as close to a coincidence as we ever came. Melvin Williams had a coincidence once but he was in Paducah when he had it.

After the hunting dog was run over, Elvira turned her affection to cats. She never forgave me for running over her cat. With a lawn mower. The cat died nine times in one revolution. And left enough guitar strings for Peter, Paul and Mary.

For a revival we had to have an evangelist. An evangelist was a preacher who had come from far enough away that we didn't know not to believe him. At the end of every service the evangelist called on people to repent and join the church. Those who came to the front of the church to repent were asked how they came. You can join a Baptist Church on a profession of your faith, by a letter from another Baptist Church saying they didn't hold anything against you, or on your own statement that you were once a member of a Baptist Church but attended so rarely no one could remember you well enough to vote against you.

When Joyce Cashion joined the church, the evangelist asked her, "How do you come?" Joyce said, "I came by Studebaker."

There was lots of singing at a revival and we got to sing songs that weren't in the hymnal. The song leader taught them to us and we'd sing them every night. Biddy Boatright loved to sing but she couldn't remember the words so she wrote them in the book in which she collected recipes. One night when the music began Biddie reached into her purse, grabbed her book and sang, "Three cups of sugar, two cups of flour..."

We had hay rides. On a Baptist hay ride all the hay was inside the horse. All the boys were on one side of the wagon and all the girls on the other, with a row of deacons between them. I did hold hands with Myrtle Bagley on a hayride but I was in Genesis and she was in Revelations. When I got to Romans she was in Lamentations. We never did reach the interbiblical period.

People used to think Baptists knew the Bible, but shoot, that was just so we'd know where to get together. "I'll meet you in Habakkuk." Our senior year two Baptists had to get married because they were caught in the Acts. Just before Exodus.

The Methodists had "brush arbor" revivals. A brush arbor was a scaffold with mesquite limbs thrown over it. Mesquite limbs weren't much of a shade so they used it only at night. I asked the Baptist pastor why, if they were outside at night, the Methodists needed to be under anything. He said it was the same reason Methodists slept under a sheet even when it was hot. Methodists had a lot to hide. Some people came to brush arbor revivals that wouldn't come to church. Like Old Man Blevins. Old Man Blevins had an orange dog that he called Red. Blevins was a Baptist but he didn't go anywhere without Red and the Baptists wouldn't let him bring Red in the church. He attended Methodist brush arbor revivals though because they let Red sit at his feet.

Well, that made some of the Baptist boys mad, Old Man Blevins not going to the Baptist Church like we had to and going to a Methodist revival. What made the Methodist boys mad was that midway through the sermon, Blevins always got up in the middle of the service, walked around the corner of the church which was right beside the brush arbor and relieved himself.

To teach him a lesson, the Methodist boys enticed one of the Baptist boys to slip up beside Old Man Blevins in the dark and slap him on the exposed part of his anatomy. Which I did. It didn't teach him a lesson, though. He just waved his hand and said, "Get away, Red."

I, however, did learn a lesson. I learned three lessons. Stay away from Methodist services. Don't interfere with other people's business. And watch out for old Red.

Miracles in Chillicothe ⟶

Chillicothe was so small there was only one Baptist Church. But Chillicothe was big enough for anyone who was a Christian. In addition to the Baptist Church, there was a Church of Christ and a whole other church for nothing but Methodists.

We didn't have any of the deviate religions that serve wine in church. We didn't want alcohol and/or Presbyterians inside the county line. As for Unitarians, we had heard of them. We had heard of UFOs. We allowed that they might exist, but we believed Unitarians were more likely to visit Roswell than Chillicothe.

We had all the diversity that God required and good sense permitted. Which was two more churches than Chillicothe had stores. Although we separated into three different buildings to worship God, we were ecumenical. We got together at school, football games and Modeen's Home Cafe. We even visited each other's churches. Sometimes. For most, it was a once in a lifetime experience. Wedding, funeral or vandalism.

I, like other good Christians in Chillicothe, worshipped in the Baptist Church. We were God-loved and God-favored but we tried not to lord it over God's lesser children. Except on the school board, the city council and the Chamber of Commerce.

Other than God's favor and majority power, there weren't many differences between the churches. The Church of Christ didn't have a piano and didn't want one. We had a piano but it went out of tune every time the weather changed and in north-west Texas the weather changed every day. Sometimes several times a day. Sometimes during the choir special. The pianist was adamant about that.

The Methodists had stained glass windows; we had venetian blinds. The Methodists had a pipe organ and were vain about it. We had a baptistery—the Methodists didn't have a baptistery—but we weren't vain about it. We let them use it any time they wanted.

The perfidious Methodists said the Baptists coveted their pipe organ and that covetousness was forbidden in the Ten Commandments. Every Baptist who had been to Sunday School knew that. We also knew it was at the far end where things didn't matter so much. Brother Whatley said the really bad things were at the front end of the list—swearing, wearing a crucifix, and going to the picture show on Sunday.

Killing was wrong unless done in the name of national security, economic opportunity, or to deter violence. Adultery and not tithing were always wrong. Although tithing was not one of the original Ten. Brother Whatley said it was an oversight on God's part. Brother Whatley said that in a capitalist society covetousness was pretty much okay because if Christians didn't covet, especially at Christmas and Easter, the economy would collapse. Besides, we didn't covet the Methodist's pipe organ. We envied their air of superiority because they had a pipe organ.

The pipe organ was the genesis of religious dissension in Chillicothe. Church elders say that before the Methodists bought a pipe organ, Christians greeted each other as brothers, every man thinking more highly of others than of himself. The churches existed in perfect harmony and, if not purity, at least parity.

The Church of Christ didn't believe in music, not even good singing. Which was evident to everyone who passed by their church. We Baptists used a piano the way God intended and King James approved. But when the Methodists hired a graduate of McMurray College to play their pipe organ their vanity was revealed. As every good Christian knows, vanity is a sin like envy, that God forgives and other Christians overlook as long as it does not exhibit itself. The Methodists paraded their degreed organist the way they paraded their stained glass windows. Placing them so that they faced the Baptist Church. That's why we bought venetian blinds.

The Methodists sent an announcement to the Baptist Church, the Church of Christ and the Masonic Lodge. "Brothers and sis-

ters in Christ, please join us at the Methodist Church to welcome
our new college-trained organist, DeWayne Debois, who can't
wait to get his hands on our organ."

I went to the organ recital, thinking it was the Methodist
equivalent of a Baptist revival. DeWayne Debois came in, sat at
the organ and began to play. He played all five stanzas. I waited
until he finished and began another song before I fidgeted. Another song with five stanzas. Maybe six. I looked at the back of
the church to see if people were still coming in. I looked around
for the preacher, for the choir. I looked at the person beside me
who managed that benevolent smile that only Methodists and
hair stylists can master.

I asked him, "When is it going to start?"

There was no preaching, no praying, no baptisms, no collect-
ing of a love offering. Like most Methodist affairs, it never started.
It was nothing but organ music for an hour. Some members of
the Church of Christ were so offended by the Methodists' pipe
organ that they skipped church and went to Wanderer Creek to
shoot geese. And God blessed them more than the law allowed.

While plucking geese, they thanked God for his bounty and
pointed out that it was Methodist music that prevented them
from attending the Church of Christ, in some mysterious way
that only God could understand. Then they got to talking about
what they, and God, could do with the goose down. They packed
it in pillow cases and Saturday night before Christmas, they
sneaked into the Methodist Church and stuffed the down in the
organ pipes.

On Sunday morning DeWayne Debois launched into "Angels We Have Heard on High" with all the stops out. The Methodists were astounded by a heavenly cloud like the one that guided
the Hebrews in the desert. Those Methodists who were devout
kneeled at the altar. Everyone except those three sat in their pews
sucking in feathers with each breath. Every time one of them
sneezed a holy down devil danced before his eyes.

The Church of Christ, Methodist and Baptist Churches were
located on opposite sides of the same intersection, the way Rexall,

Walgreens and Eckerds locate close to each other in a spirit of fellowship and goodwill. That Sunday morning when the Baptists emerged from church they were awestruck at the way the Holy Spirit had visited the Methodists. The hair of some Methodists had turned white in contrition. Others were beginning to fledge out like squabs. The Church of Christ preacher ran across the street. He peeked inside and burst into tears when he discovered that the Methodist Church was where God's angels went to molt.

Some Baptists were slow to forgive the Methodist presumption in arrogating the Holy Spirit to themselves because of one fluffy visitation. We knew who they were. They were nothing but a bunch of liberals who promoted school dances. Football was the only contact sport we allowed.

Opa Lee Ballard was as straight-backed a Baptist as you would ever hope to see outside of Abilene. Then one of those Methodist feathers got down the back of her dress, right down there between the Baptist, the Methodist, and the Church of Christ. Opa Lee had to pretend she was organizing her purse while wiggling her behind. She grabbed her hair brush and brushed her hair, continuing well below her waist, snagging the threads on her best J.C. Penny church meeting dress, and unraveling her rump.

Opa Lee, who every day prayed for people she didn't know in lands she would never see, couldn't find it in her heart to forgive the Methodists for her disheveled derriere.

Opa Lee had two daughters, Gladys and Baby Girl. She raised them in the Baptist Church and taught them the duties of a child to her parents. Gladys, the older daughter served her father until his death and continued to serve her mother. Baby Girl, the younger daughter, married a Methodist. DeWayne Debois, who had a personality pompadour, with a character curl and hair of a suspicious color.

Opa Lee went to the shower given for Baby Girl by the Baptist Church Women's Missionary Auxiliary, but she would not eat the Lottie Moon lime sherbet or drink the Annie Armstrong pineapple punch. She sat crying in a corner. When Baby Girl began opening the presents, Opa Lee sobbed, "I want to thank you all for praying for my daughter. I don't blame you for this. God lets Methodists get away with anything. Sprinkling. That pipe organ. A college-trained organist. Baby Girl never thought about boys until she heard DeWayne play. And saw his arrangement."

Opal Lee and Gladys did not attend the wedding. They refused all invitations to visit Baby Girl, and would not permit DeWayne DeBois inside their lonely and heartbroken house. Rejected, Baby Girl and DeWayne moved to Oklahoma and fell into a life of Methodist living. As the years passed and Opa Lee became old, Gladys catered to her every wish, reading to her from the Baptist Hymnal and reporting the aggravations of the Methodist Church. Baby Girl continued her life of Methodist living among the Okla-homicidal. Then one day Gladys called her sister and said, "Come home, Baby Girl. Mother is dying."

Leaving their children in the care of her husband, Baby Girl came home for the first time since her marriage. Gladys ran to greet her. For a time the two sisters clung to each other, shedding tears over the years they had lost, and Baby Girl's children that Gladys and her mother had never seen. Baby Girl asked to see her mother. With trepidation, Gladys invited Baby Girl into the house she had not been in since the day of her wedding. They tiptoed upstairs to Opa Lee's bedroom and Gladys timidly knocked on her door. There was no response but Gladys opened the door and she and Baby Girl stepped inside Opa Lee's dark and cheerless room.

The old woman opened her eyes, looked in amazement upon Baby Girl and motioned for Gladys to approach. Gladys hoped that with her dying breath, her mother would thank her for the life Gladys had sacrificed in order to care for her parents. She feared her mother would scold her for allowing her prodigal sister into the house. She prayed her mother would forgive Baby Girl. She suspected her mother would pass on a final bit of Baptist philosophy.

Gladys kneeled beside the dying woman and turned her ear to hear her mother's last whispers. "Guard your purse," her mother said. "There are Methodists in the house."

Time changes human hearts and it came to pass that the Baptist Church needed a church secretary. This was a problem in a small church in a small town because a secretary would be privy to much of the same information as the pastor, who often illustrated his sermons by saying, "A member of the congregation came to see me this week about his wife.

"He came home from work early and found her sitting at the kitchen table, in her nightie, reading a romance. And I want to tell that woman," he said, pointing at the woman and the three women sitting behind her, "that God doesn't want to see her in her nightie, reading a romance. The first thing you know a woman like that will be lying in bed, smoking cigarettes and reading Cosmopolitan. God doesn't want that. God wants her at the kitchen table, submitting to her husband."

Baptist women were too busy washing dishes and tending children at home and tending dishes and washing children at church to accept a paying position at the church. Methodist women were too busy lying in bed, smoking cigarettes and reading Cosmo. And, everyone knew a Methodist secretary would talk down to any Baptist who called the church, even a deacon. In the Methodist kindergarten they taught children to say, good, gooder, goodest. Bad, badder, Baptist. Matter, mother, Methodist.

God did not want men becoming church secretaries. Start that and the first thing you know, they would want to prepare Wednesday night suppers and clean up afterwards. That left the Church of Christ, where women were trained in the way men would have them go. Or, the unchurched where women went without bras. And God did not want to see a bra-less woman answering the telephone in a Baptist Church.

The Baptist Church hired Vernell Thomas, a member of the Church of Christ. But before she was hired as secretary, Vernell had to stand before the Baptist congregation, in a bra, and, of course, a blouse and jacket over it. And vow on a King James Baptist Bible not to repeat gossip. And she didn't.

She called Maude Foster and said, "Did you hear what happened to Chip Spence?"

"No," Maude said.

Vernell said, "I better not tell you, but it was real bad."

Maude called Vinnie, and Vinnie called Rachel, and Rachel called Maida, and Maida called Chip's mother and Chip's mother called Chip. After denying that anything had happened to him, good or bad, Chip confessed he had lost his red-letter edition Bible, with split-cowhide binding, that his mother had given him on his twelfth birthday. And the whole church breathed a sigh of relief. That he hadn't lost his gear box and moved to Quanah.

Then Vernell called Maude and said, "Maude, did you hear where Chip Spence lost his Bible? Then I better not tell you." And Maude called Vinnie, and Vinnie called Rachel, and Rachel called Maida, and Maida called Chip's mother, and Chip's mother called Chip, and Chip confessed he had lost his Bible in the Church of Christ. And the whole church breathed a sigh of relief. That Chip hadn't lost his Bible in the pool hall. With chalk marks on the split-cowhide binding. That still looked like new.

Then Vernell called Maude and said, "Did you hear who Chip was sitting with when he lost his Bible in the Church of Christ?" And Maude called, and Vinnie called, and Rachel called, and Maida called, and Chip's mother called, and Chip confessed he was sitting with a widow woman. With two children. Newly arrived from Crowell. Where she attended the Assembly of God. And the whole church breathed a sigh of relief that Chip wasn't sitting with a Methodist.

Then Vernell called Maude and said, "Did you hear why Chip was sitting with a widow woman when he lost his Bible in the Church of Christ?" And Maude, and Vinnie, and Rachel, and Maida, and Chip's mother. And Chip confessed the widow woman was church shopping and would visit the Baptist Church with him next Sunday. The Baptists breathed a sigh of relief that Chip was doing missionary work in the Assembly of God. The members of the Church of Christ breathed a sigh of relief that Vernell did not gossip. The Methodists sighed.

That's the Gospel in Chillicothe, where good people go to church. People who love their neighbor go to the Baptist Church.

People who love polyester attend the Church of Christ. And the perfidious Methodists listen to organ music, knowing it is as close to heaven as they will ever get. Amen and amen.

A Baptist Looks Askance ~

Recently a former pastor of mine said, "I may not be a Baptist much longer." I said, "I may not be a Baptist much longer either." We both said the same thing ten years ago. Fifteen years ago. Twenty years ago. That kind of statement is Baptistic. Belief in the church as the body of Christ and a healthy concern over what portion of that body is locally represented.

Baptist beliefs are usually defined by others in negative terms. No dancing. No drinking. No smiles for two miles after church.

Baptists do not really believe that we are the only ones who will go to heaven. We believe that for the first time in our church lives we will sit in the front row.

We do not believe that John the Baptist started the first Baptist church. We do believe that if there had been a Baptist Church, Jesus would have gone there. And not been caught associating with people like Judas. Thomas. Peter. James and John.

Warren G. Harding was a Baptist. So was Harry Truman, Jimmy Carter and Bill Clinton. Nat Turner was a Baptist preacher, as was Adam Clayton Powell and Martin Luther King, Jr. Baptists are also prominent in the Ku Klux Klan, white supremacy and anti-government groups. Historically non-conformist and anti-establishment Baptists today get along with everyone except other Baptists.

Some Baptists are free-will, others are Calvinistic, some believe in apostasy, some believe in open communion, some believe in baptism by immersion only, some believe in the verbal inspiration of the Bible, some believe there are no mistakes in the Bible, some believe in the virgin birth of Jesus, some believe in the virgin birth of themselves, some believe in the premillennial return of Christ, some have women deacons, some have women clergy. Landmark Baptists believe they are the only true church and the first Christian church was the First Baptist Church of Jerusalem, Landmark. Seventh Day Baptists worship on Saturday. Free Will Baptists practice foot washing.

What unites these people? I am not so naive as to think that Baptists practice what they say they believe. Any more than Presbyterians practice what they say they believe. Or Masons. Or Communists. Or the Christian Coalition.

Baptists do hold some common beliefs. One is believer's baptism. No one is to be baptized until she, alone, without spiritual guides and ecclesiastical authorities has encountered God and been transformed through the power of Jesus Christ. This belief has led to an emphasis on an ecstatic moment and a neglect of the faithful life. Baptists tend to see the Christian life as event rather than process.

This emphasis on evangelism, on confrontation has resulted in enormous growth by Baptists—a growth in numbers which is not always sustained by intellectual and spiritual development. I will try not to infer a relationship between intellectual and spiritual development and Baptist diversity.

Baptists say they believe in the priesthood of the believer, that no one needs any one but Jesus in order to approach God, find forgiveness and salvation, and discover God's revelation through the Bible. We talk about the fellowship of believers, the communion of the saints, the tie that binds, but we believe you stand alone before God. We say that Jesus is not the answer for you unless you have found that answer for yourself, that Baptist doctrine is not the right doctrine for you unless you have hammered that faith out of your own experience with grace. Harry Truman said, "I'm a Baptist; no one can tell me what to believe."

Baptists believe in the soul competency of the individual, that the individual is free to believe or not to believe without any interference from authority, particularly government authority. Some Baptists want a wall of separation between church and state; other Baptists prefer a one-way door through which they may pass in order to plunder the public treasury and require public reform without the government being able to pass through in order to require taxes or accountability.

Baptists say they have no creed except the Bible. Every person is competent to read and interpret the Bible for herself. Without the interference of any authority. After which she will look for others holding common beliefs and find them in a building which has Baptist across the front. Landmark Baptist. Or Free Will Baptist. Or Bible Baptist. Or Seventh Day, General Six-Principle, Primitive, Particular, Regular, Fundamentalist, Conservative, Southern, Northern, Finnish, Hungarian, French, Italian, Polish, or Three Peas In A Pod Baptist Church.

Such freedom should ensure a denomination of theologians. Instead, it guarantees a denomination of traditionalists. Whatever was believed in the past has to be right, and most likely was complete. Baptist seminaries lead all others in the number of theological students but Baptists have produced no theologians who are influential or even read outside our denomination. The past, if not prelude, is prison.

Baptists say they believe in the autonomy of the local church. The local church is a democracy that, directed by the Holy Spirit, receives members, ordains clergy, and determines its own theological position and moral stance. There is no visible hierarchy, and no outside person can tell that church what to do. The president of the United States or of the Southern Baptist Convention cannot tell a small Baptist church in Oregon or Arkansas to accept black members, female ministers, or not to fire its pastor. Baptists are sometimes in the news because some local church votes to become Pentecostal, or Church of Christ, or to sell the building and sit on a mountain, or votes to censure a book, an idea, a practice, another Baptist Church, its pastor or half its own membership.

Flynns are Irish Catholic. Originally from County Cork, fourteen came to Texas to build the Fort Worth and Denver Railroad. Life in Texas was so rough, all but three of them went to Connecticut. Of those who remained in Texas, one died of the fever, my grandfather was murdered, my grandmother hunkered down with three young sons on a homestead near Chillicothe.

There were few Catholics in West Texas and no churches in Chillicothe. When my grandmother and her children attended services, they listened to preaching by a Methodist circuit rider. My father's two brothers became Methodists. My father was suspicious of organized religion and hostile to the church.

My mother was from a long line of Methodist preachers, her mother and father being the only Baptists in the family. The only Baptist relatives I have are my mother, my sister and my brother who is a Baptist minister. And they say, "I don't know if I'll be a Baptist much longer."

My mother took us to church every Sunday. Because we lived four miles from Chillicothe, when the roads were muddy or iced over or washed out, Dad drove us to town and waited at the fire station until church was over, then drove us home.

I generally believed what I heard in church. Stones were God's gift to little men. Kings were God's gift to bad women. Shepherds washed their flocks by night. I wasn't sure what a flock was but I figured shepherds had a good reason for washing them in the dark.

I became a Baptist but I wasn't vain about it. My brother, for some unknown reason, became an advocate of twice on Sunday. He walked or hitchhiked the four miles to church every Sunday evening. My sister was not tempted, but I began going with him. One, he started thinking he was better than I was. I couldn't permit that. Two, I noticed this girl who went to church on Sunday night. I wasn't old enough to date so the best I could do was to sit beside her in church and draw funny faces in the hymnal. I didn't attract much attention from the girl, but I was noticed by the adults who remarked what a good boy I was. Before getting in their cars and driving away, leaving me and my brother to walk four miles home.

I desperately needed to be noticed. I wanted to be recognized for what I was. I didn't know what I was but I needed someone to see it and give me credit for it. My only accomplishment in school was to be first in my class to get pimples and the last to get rid of them.

I played football. That is, I played between games. I wasn't the All-District tackle. I was the dummy the All-District tackle tackled. "He's going to hurt one of our starters," the coach said, turning to me during scrimmage. "Go in there and let him hurt you."

I was a passive scholar, preferring to lie in wait and attack homework only in self-defense. No one could convince me that God invented algebra.

The only talent I seemed to have was—I was good at being good. I excelled at not swearing (I was too shy), not drinking (I lived in a dry county), not smoking (I was too cheap to buy my own and too shy to ask for anyone else's), not dancing (I was too cheap to take my own and too shy to ask for anyone else's) and not deviating from the rocky path of being poor, thirteen, and without a driver's license.

Being good required some luck. I was a teenager before television. I had no one to teach me how to be a smart-mouthed, sex-obsessed rebel. My father and mother were so old as to be beyond temptation. Everyone in Chillicothe knew my parents and reported when I entertained temptation. "I saw Robert looking at Sunshine Magazine in the drug store." Sunshine Magazine, that promoted nudity through argument rather than photography, was the closest thing to Playboy we had.

I also had the ability to look humble while being tackled by a two-hundred pound social misfit, and a personality that girls found resistible. In Sunday School we debated which was more desirable—personality or character. With my personality I didn't need character.

Without intending it I discovered I had become the perfect Baptist. I didn't contemplate what was good, true or beautiful, but I did a near-perfect imitation of a dead stick.

And I got the same degree of attention. To be noticed, in addition to being good, I had to look good. Something besides sitting in the car with my date outside the gym, boycotting the school prom.

Needing to look good, I decided to attend a college that was good at looking good. And Baylor accepted me. At Baylor everybody was good at looking good. There were All America football players who ran with Jesus, and All America basketball players who dribbled for God. A runner-up for Miss America who said, "I'd rather be a rose in God's garden than a thorn in man's flesh." Former drug addicts who got high on Jesus, and former street gang leaders who hung out with The Man.

It was obvious that if I was going to look good I had to do something spectacular. I declared war on North Korea. I dropped out of college and enlisted in the Marines. I was going to kill a Commie for Christ. I didn't know what I was but the Marines knew and they told me. In a vocabulary that was refreshingly new. I was a whore for the Corps.

After the Marines I returned to Baylor sans even a Good Conduct Medal. No one had missed me. No one knew I was gone. No one noticed how good I looked in uniform. Medals wouldn't have helped. Most students thought Korea was a government plot to prevent the media from noticing Friday Night Missions. At Friday Night Missions students held street services for drunks, derelicts and drama professors.

Upon my return to Baylor, two people did notice me. Paul Baker and Eugene McKinney thought I had a gift. They thought everyone had a gift. That was beside the point. They thought I had one. It wouldn't make me look good but I could use it to do good. Here was a new concept. Instead of doing something spectacular to look good I could use the humble gift God gave me to do good.

Baker and McKinney thought I could write. "I'm from Chillicothe," I explained, shamefaced. Folks from Chillicothe couldn't write. They didn't even read. "I'm from Hereford," Baker said. Hereford was almost as small and far smellier than Chillicothe but Baker had brought the attention of the world to the Baylor Theater.

"I didn't say you could write well, I said you could write," McKinney explained.

They were from the accursed drama department. That didn't matter. They said I could write. They gave me permission to use my gift to do good. I was like a lame man who was told to walk. I didn't want to walk; I wanted to dance, to run, to leap. First I needed a wilderness experience, an apprenticeship in Hell. I enrolled at Southwestern Baptist Theological Seminary.

At Southwestern, my professors were like guards at an art museum who defended treasures they hardly enjoyed. They knew names, dates, prices but the glory escaped them. Their eyes were on us. Don't touch. Don't stand so close. Don't examine the brush strokes. Don't study how the artist envisioned and constructed the painting. Don't try to replicate the work. Just accept how valuable it is.

I was being trained as equipment for the church, as uniform and replaceable as the office typewriter. I tried to explain to my professors that I wanted to examine the treasure, to explore it, to immerse myself in its poetry, to dance to its song. To discover the mind behind the words. The overworked professors listened with benign impatience. Just do like everyone else. Humble yourself and worship The Treasure. At least this copy of it.

If you believe God gave the writers the words they wrote, then you don't need to examine the writers' struggle through doubt, despair, death, disease in their world and in their lives to find a God who was revealing himself. The only thing that mattered was God's word choices.

The scrutiny of word choices, the selection of isolated sentences in the Bible instead of studying the meaning and purpose of the writer is the source of most of the disputes, persecutions, murders and wars among Christians. Is "this is my blood" literal? Is "if your eye causes you to offend pluck it out" figurative? Is it consubstantiation or transubstantiation? Is it a young maiden or a virgin who will bear a son? Is it "sell all you have and give it to the poor" or "you must be born again" that is the way to heaven?

The belief that the Bible was authored by God without the intrusion or adulteration of human minds and human language— that the whole must be equally venerated, Numbers as authoritative as Isaiah, Deuteronomy as revered as Psalms, the Epistle of

Jude as significant as the Gospel of John, the Song of Songs as useful as Genesis because no part of God is inferior; that there is no need to read or understand the Bible in terms of human personalities and historical circumstances because God is timeless—that belief is idolatry.

I didn't understand all that at the time. I knew only that there was no intellectual excitement, no creative stimulus. I had neither the guts nor the ego to say I wanted to be a writer, especially that I wanted to be a writer like the author of Job or the Gospel of John. My professors believed it was sinful pride to think that I had a gift or that anyone needed it. Baptists believed in confrontation and proclamation.

"What is Baptist art?" I asked. Why, it was a painting of Jesus, or at least Moses, and illustrated a story. Jesus knocking at the door. Moses carrying two chunks of stone. "Could a devout Baptist paint a religious painting that didn't represent earthly or heavenly things and didn't illustrate a story?" Of course not. The problem with belief in the freedom of the individual conscience is that it tends to make some Baptists authorities on everything. The sovereign conscience does not wish to be troubled with the facts.

The problem with having no hierarchy, no visible power structure is that it lends itself to personality cults and demagoguery. In a Baptist church, the vote of every member counts the same—the vote of a woman the same as that of a man, the vote of a twelve-year-old the same as that of the pastor. However, the voices are not the same. To be heard one must have authority and authority is the ultimate end of looking good.

A charismatic Baptist leader can determine orthodoxy for his church, perhaps even his denomination. A coalition of such authorities can direct what will and what will not be taught in Baptist colleges and seminaries and who may teach there.

Private matters may become denominational concerns. And social concerns may become private matters. The way to combat pornography, alcohol, bingo, is to legislate it out of existence. The way to combat injustice, hunger, racism, war, is to confront an individual with the gospel.

I wanted to do good. Not to proclaim but to imply. Not to promote but to evoke. Not to indoctrinate but to question. I wrote but no one noticed. Just as Baptists have produced few theologians to examine and challenge our faith, we have produced few artists to explore and broaden our understanding of our religious and spiritual selves. Or to represent us accurately and honestly to those who do not share our faith.

Faith in confrontation and proclamation has created doubt in indirection. Art is indirect. Art permits, even provokes, deliberate ambiguity. Indirection and ambiguity are a challenge to authority. There is nothing indirect or ambiguous about the Ten Commandments. That's why we wish the Ten Commandments posted on the walls of schools and court houses rather than the Sermon on the Mount.

But wait! The Ten Commandments, while writ on stone, are hardly categorical. What are "other gods?" Is a coin a graven image? A statue of David? A statue of Jesus? A painting of the creation? When is the Sabbath and how do you keep it holy? Does "Thou shalt not kill" exclude war? Capital punishment? Euthanasia? Does "Thou shalt not steal, covet, bear false witness" exempt Manifest Destiny? Capitalism? Advertising? Politics? There are good reasons for guarding treasures rather than examining them.

The Sermon on the Mount left us with more questions than answers. Jesus expected us to seek the answers but he didn't expect us to know it all. However, to be an authority one must know-it-all. Know-it-alls are comforting to those who don't want to play hide-and-seek with God, but scream to the sky, "Just give me the answers." Know-it-alls are scary to those who believe the spiritual voyage is from darkness to light through clouds of obscurity, waves of doubt, storms of pride, the wrecked hulks of Quit, Tired, and Let Someone Else Do It.

For those who believe truth is in the voyage and not the harbor, it would be comforting to have charts, buoys, and lighthouses from those who floundered before them. Like the lighthouses left by Jeremiah, Amos, Tolstoy, Mozart, Van Gogh.

I think it must be wonderful to be Jewish and to have a rich tradition in art, music and literature expressing what it means to be Jewish. It must be edifying to be able to reaffirm one's identity and to expand one's experience in the words of Saul Bellow, Bernard Malamud, Chaim Potok.

Christians do have a marvelous heritage through the work of Beethoven, Michelangelo, Dostoyevsky. It is a treasure many Baptists have scarcely examined. We know the names, the dates, the prices.

It may be possible to do good while looking good but it is probably impossible to do good as a writer and to be an authority. An authority knows the answer before she raises the question. A writer asks the question in order to seek the answer knowing that the answer may be that there is no answer. Or that the answer is unknowable.

I don't write about Baptists, or Protestants, or even Christians. I want to write about mankind. To explore what it means to be a person in the time of the nonperson. What it means to be a human being in a corporate world where the importance of an individual depends on the power of the organization to which she belongs. I want to be alien to nothing that is human, whether it be joy or pain. To be exempt from neither doubt nor desperation.

I want to cast myself into the raging sea of life. To discover that the Master of the Sea is the Lord of Life. And to emerge to tell the story. Although it may be ambiguous, more parable than platitude. And I might not emerge a Baptist.

A Sense of Place ⟶

Bob: If you're from Chillicothe, Texas, sometimes you get the feeling it's not a real place. It's one of those hallucinations folks have. Like Albuquerque. People have heard of Albuquerque. There are some people who say they have actually seen Albuquerque, although everyone knows its not a real place. "Chillicothe," folks say. "Never heard of it." "Have you ever driven from Fort Worth to Amarillo?" "Lots of times," they say. "Then you drove through it." "Never saw it," they say.

Maybe the reason Chillicothe isn't real is because Chillicothe doesn't have much reason for existence. The only reason it's there is to give folks from Vernon and Quanah something to feel superior about. It's not a real place like Jacksboro that has history, and a Fort, and a courthouse. The Green Frog Cafe.

Joyce: Yes, it's true. Jacksboro is superior. You mentioned driving through Chillicothe. One could not and still cannot drive through Jacksboro. One must drive around it. In addition to the other amenities you have just named such as Fort Richardson, the places known for fine cuisine and a courthouse, the town is built on a square. You simply cannot trust any town that is not build on a square. A square speaks of antiquity, of stability, and the shape of a town's personality.

Bob: Yeah, but if you were from Chillicothe you didn't have to put on airs. You didn't have to pretend you knew how to spell Chillicothe. No one else knew either. Not even the politicians could pronounce it.

Joyce: We knew how to spell Jacksboro and we knew how to pronounce it. The word was misspelled however. It is spelled J-A-C-K-S-B-O-R-O, but the correct enunciation is "Jackspur" as in "the spur belonging to the boot of Jack." That is why the town was so named. We were educated about such historical matters early in Jacksboro. We were smart.

Bob: In real places like Jacksboro, smart kids rode to school on long buses. Dumb kids rode to school on short buses. In Chillicothe, everybody rode a short bus.

But Chillicothe was better than Jacksboro because when you told your folks there was nothing to do, they didn't argue with you. They couldn't find anything to do either. Dad used to spend whole days straightening fence staples. "What're you doing, dad?" "I'm straightening these steeples." "Don't they have to bend over the bob wire?" "I'll bend them back when I get ready to fix the fence."

I've spent whole days watching dad straighten staples. I'd get awfully hungry before dad would stop so mother could fix us something to eat. Then we'd go to the house and watch her slice onions. She also sliced tomatoes but with onions you had participatory viewing. I guess those were the happiest days of my life, watching dad straighten staples all day and then watching mother slice onions. And it was educational. It prepared me for watching television.

Joyce: Watching staple bending and onion peeling. That is— narrow. In Jacksboro, we watched each other and we listened and that was truly educational, hands on learning, you know. I first learned my colors from people. Mondays were big days. We inspected each other's wash on the line and reported if the socks were *gray*. I heard a man say once, "Oh, some widows do look good in *black*." The widow Jones wore *red* soon after her husband's death and the consoling deacons said she had a peace that passed all understanding. All boys had *green* teeth, and *black*-dog-breath. And the Ag boys said Mrs. Jacobs Sunday dress was the color of chicken-do. (We didn't use the S word except "shucks, shoot, and ah, shaw," and who wants to say chicken-shucks or bull-shaw.) That meant the color was kind of a cross between *yellow* and *green* with some *brown* thrown in depending on what the chicken had been pecking and where. Never wear *white* shoes before Easter nor after Labor Day. But you don't have to wear shoes at all from June to August, if you don't want to. And many-colored rainbows proved to me that God always kept his promises and that Jacksboro, which was neither on a river or a lake and certainly not situated on a low place, would never again be destroyed by flood—at least the square never would, which was all that counted.

You might not have had anything to do in Chillicothe but we certainly did. I had my hands full just learning my colors.

Bob: You may have learned your colors, and I do admire your chicken-do dress but you don't seem to recognize any shape but square. Chillicothe didn't have a square. Infrequent visitors looked in vain for what was generally known as town. "Where's town?" "You're standing right in the middle of it." "But where is it?" Like Oakland, there was no "there" there. Chillicothe was long. But not very long.

Chillicothe doesn't appear on post cards because by the time they wrote Chillicothe there was no room for Texas. And no one ever sent a telegram.

Chillicothe has a road sign. They hired a painter to paint the road sign, but he was one of those painters who moved his lips when he read. Since no tourist ever slowed down when they got to Chillicothe the painter put the sign longways, parallel to the road so folks would have time to read it as they passed by. Which was okay except that the whole town was between the L and the O.

Joyce: Chillicothe is certainly a strange place, a rectangular place, a strung out place. What did you do for entertainment?

Bob: For entertainment you could go to church and be told you were wicked or you could stay home and feel good about yourself. We were Baptists. We couldn't feel good about ourselves even when we stayed home. So a lot of Sundays we just went to church. Ministers could be entertaining though. Especially Brother Whatley whose favorite sermon was on the sin of fornification. Every time he said fornification he wet his lips. He made it sound so appealing that boys dropped out of school and joined the Marines so they could get fornified.

Joyce: Regular Sunday Church wasn't especially entertaining to me, and I was a Baptist too. I had to look to other churches for entertainment. Revivals were about as much entertainment as we could hold up to but since revivals happened in the summer time we had a spell to recover. We got a look at the ways of the heathen brothers and sisters in other denominations. I liked it when the Methodists entertained. You know, don't you that the Methodists were responsible for all those bloody songs? Oh, I know we Baptists sang them and tried to pretend that Fanny J. Crosby wrote everything, but I found out later that it was the Wesley boys who were responsible for all that bloody business. You remember—"Alas, and did my Savior bleed;" "Are you washed in the blood of the Lamb?" "And that thy blood was shed for me." "There is a fountain filled with blood drawn from Emanuel's veins." And what about "Blessed Assurance" which says "born of his spirit, washed in his blood?"

Bob: Joyce, Fanny Crosby wrote "Blessed Assurance."

Joyce: Well, it doesn't matter who wrote it. The Baptists had a right to blame somebody else for something some of the time.

Testifying was even more entertaining than revival music. At revival time, the preacher would call for the testifying and then anyone who wanted to could get up and tell about the sinning he had been doing and how Jesus had washed away his sins, in blood, of course. None of us children ever testified because we were too young to know about hard sinning, but we could tell from the testifying that we had a lot to look forward to.

We played games too, for entertainment. And not just at church. Didn't you play games in Chillicothe?

Bob: We played mumbly peg, and Blind Man's Butt.

Joyce: Spin the Bottle, Knocking for Love, and Post Office.

Bob: Those were girls games. We played Hide and Seek, Red Rover and Pop the Wimp.

Joyce: Hearts, Rummy, Dominoes.

Bob: We didn't go in much for games, but we had mysteries. Our biggest mystery happened in the high school cafeteria. There were always two things on your plate you couldn't identify. One was a meat and one wasn't.

Of course when things got real dull we could always go to the big city for entertainment. We used to go to Vernon at least once a month. In Vernon you could spend all day in the White's Auto just looking around. My dad used to take me for walks through the town. The court house to use the toilet. The gin, the grain elevators. The court house to use to toilet. There's something about being in the city that excites the kidneys.

One time dad took me for a walk in the Vernon cemetery, only it wasn't called the Vernon cemetery, it was called the Yamparika cemetery. That should have told me something right there. City folks named their cemetery after a perfume. We got to looking at the gravestones and there were angels, and wooly lambs, and petrified trees. And some of the stones had stories on them. We got to reading the stories about how God came and got Aunt Martha and took her away. It got dark while we were reading about God coming and taking Aunt Martha, and scary, and the angels started looking like maybe God sent them to take me away and I got scared.

I got to looking around to see if God was coming after me and a little dog jumped on my leg. Only I didn't know it was a little dog. Today I know it was a poodle, but Chillicothe didn't go in much for poodles. If a dog didn't look like a dog we didn't believe it was a dog. We were Christians.

This dog didn't look like a dog; it looked like one of them wooly lambs and I thought it was going to drag me into a grave. I didn't say much about it to dad. I just ran. I ran across a U.S. Highway. I ran down the main street of town. I ran through a latched screen door. Leaving a permanent impression.

My mother was mad. At my dad. "You let my little boy run across the highway?" mother yelled at dad. "You let him run down the street? You let him run through a screen door?" Mother was pretty sure it was dad's fault. "Why didn't you stop him?" she screamed. "I couldn't catch him," dad said.

Joyce: See there! It has to do with towns built on a square again. If you had a square in Chillicothe, you wouldn't have to run through the screen door. You could have run around the square. There would have been plenty of folks to stop you. You could have got help; maybe somebody would have counseled you, guided you, violated you; maybe the Ku Klux Klan would have been in the midst of a burning and you would have had light to see by. You wouldn't have had to run plumb through a screen door. You would have been calm when you got home. You would have known that nothing in the cemetery was as death defying as life on the Jacksboro Square.

Bob: In Chillicothe the most death defying thing we had was Algebra. The only people who took Algebra were girls who were interested in comparative shopping. Chillicothe is a farming community and farming is as death defying as anybody wants to get.

Joyce: Chillicothe was just a hick farming town strung along the highway between rows of cotton or something. Jacksboro was a ranching town. Ranchers are superior to farmers. Naturally, I think it was to do with horses. Farmers walk behind horses and when you spend your days behind a plow looking at a horse's rump and trying to keep from stepping in something, it affects the way you perceive the world. But when you get to ride the horses, people look up to you. They have to even if you're four feet eight. I grew up riding horses and thinking I was taller than I really was. Some kids rode their horses to school. They tied them and let them graze on the playground. They took those animals home foot sore and limping because all of us had run out and ridden them at recess, jumped them over the see-saws, or run them in a figure eight around two merry go-rounds. That kind of training will improve the quickness in both horses and children. Jim Bob Arnold used to get his horses in shape for the round-up by letting his two boys bring the animals to school for two weeks before he gathered his steers off the range. When he did get his herd bunched, he let the Ag boys and us girls too take their pick to show at the Fort Worth Stock Show. The judges at Fort Worth had to look quick at the Jacksboro entries because the animals were so wild that it took three to get them in the ring, three more to get them out of the ring and three to run 'em down when they broke for the carnival midway. Generally, the Ag teacher just pulled the rig to one of the midway gates and waited out the show there. He never knew whether or not anybody won a ribbon. He did know that every single year he went home with more cattle than he came with. That was a kind of victory sure enough.

Bob: You were quite a girl, Joyce. In Chillicothe girls didn't know they were the opposite sex. We didn't know it either. They smelled like boys. They dressed like boys. They talked like boys. We called them little heifers. Sometimes we called them gophers. "Hey, little heifer, wanta gopher a ride? Well, saddle up the horses while I take a leak off the back porch."

Joyce: When I got to high school I discovered I was a girl. Up until that time, it was hard to tell. Riding horses and trying to rope steers on the midway does nothing to establish in your mind that men and women have different functions in the world. It didn't take me long to get the hang of it in high school. Anybody and everybody who was a girl could be a cheerleader. I feel a civic duty to share and perhaps instruct you by means of quoting some Jacksboro cheers:

Purple socks, white socks Football shoes;
We'll give Chillicothe the football blues.

Big dog, little dog,
Flop eared pup;
Jacksboro tigers
Eat 'em up.

Chillicothe Bob, long and tall;
He can pick cotton, but he can't play ball.

Harry James, Betty Grable
Come on boys, let's show 'em you're able.

Bob: Those are certainly morally edifying and ennobling, Joyce. Thank you for sharing those pearls with us swine. We didn't go in much for public screaming at Chillicothe. We were too dignified. We didn't spell out Chillicothe on the football field either. Not enough kids in school. We did spell C.H.S. But had to use lower case. Even then we had to use two dogs to make the seat of the h. They were good though. To be sure they didn't go running off, they brought in a couple of trained watch dogs that never moved. They guarded wherever they were placed. It worked great for halftime but they couldn't get them off the field and the whole second half had to be played around them. No problem though, neither team ever got to midfield. And when the game was over they picked them up with a front end loader and took them to the gin.

Joyce: Life was pretty plain in Chillicothe. Can't you name a few good things about Chillicothe?

Bob: There were a lot of good things about Chillicothe. For one thing, everybody was famous for something. I was famous for riding in the back of a pickup and roping the metals signs with house numbers that folks stuck in their yards. Until I tied on to a sign that was embedded in concrete. I tried to let go of the rope, and then I tried to ride the tail gate before I landed in the freshly oiled dirt street. After that I became the patron saint of the socially inadequate.

Joyce: That is embarrassing. You were embarrassing. I don't remember being embarrassed about anything. Everything I did was done out of a sense of knowing that I was right. Everyone in the town got embarrassed about me every summer at revival. Revivals had a strange effect on me. I don't know whether it was the music or the testifying or the preaching or what, but every time the minister asked for people to rededicate their lives, I went running off down the aisle, at every church, at every revival to give myself to whatever the Lord needed me for. I knew God was calling me and that He could help me learn whatever it was I needed to know. I bit off more than I could chew a time or two and got in a jam, especially that time the preacher called for those who would re-dedicate their lives to looking after murderers and escaped luna-tics at large who were known to be camped on the Brazos River. I was standing at the front already by the time the preacher got down to the particulars and about how we were to have our bedrolls and horses and camp gear ready by sun up. About all I heard was "To-night we camp on the Brazos de Dios." It took me awhile to get sorted out just what we were going to do after we camped.

Bob: Like you, Joyce, I thought the Lord had something special for me to do. I thought he wanted me to discover beauty. It was pretty clear that I was going to have to leave Chillicothe.

Joyce: Chillicothe isn't a pretty place, that's for certain. I have driven through it and looked between the L and the O. There aren't any trees in Chillicothe. Jacksboro is in the Western Crosstimbers. That means that there are trees, mostly oak, interspersed with rolling prairie. Trees make people feel more sure of themselves. When people have trees to get in they have a place to hide. In Chillicothe there's no place to hide. Decent people need to have secrets and a place to do things in secret. People from Chillicothe, from the Plains, are bound to be too open, too obvious, too honest, too friendly, don't you think?

Bob: I've certainly always been too honest. And I've been my share of friendly. Chillicothe is just big enough you can't forget a name. Myrtle Bailey. I always tried to forget her name. And telephone number. Somebody wrote her telephone number on the end of my belt. Every time I put on my trousers and started to buckle my belt there it was. When things go wrong call Myrtle Bailey. Myrtle Bailey fixed flats down at the Conoco and drove the wrecker and when I started driving, Dad wrote her name and telephone number inside my belt. I still think of her sometimes when I buckle my belt, and remember the way she could blow up a truck tire without using a pump.

The only person who ever forgot Myrtle Bailey's name was Brother Patrick. Old Brother Patrick had been pastor of the Baptist Church for thirty years. He had been there so long he sometimes mistook grown children for their parents. He had been pastor so long he didn't have to have help for eulogies and he didn't bother with wedding rehearsals. Until he married Ben Tooley and Sue Beach.

Old Brother Patrick looked at the two youngsters before him and got a little confused. He was pretty sure that Ben was a Tooley. You could always tell a Tooley, but you couldn't tell them much. A name came to him. David. No, David was the groom's father. Or uncle. Scott. Scott Tooley. No, Scott was a Dismuke. The Tooleys and Dismukes had married each other until the only way you could tell them apart was that the Dismukes drove Fords. The Tooleys wouldn't be caught dead in anything but a Chevrolet. There was one divorce when the new couple couldn't agree whether they would buy a Ford like his father or a Chevrolet like her mother. But usually when a Tooley and a Dismuke got married they joined the Plymouths.

The crowd in church was getting restive while Brother Patrick wrestled with the name of the bride and groom. The groom fidgeted like he was ready to bolt from the church, and the bride was on the verge of tears. Brother Patrick began a halting homily on the sacredness of marriage, hoping the names would come to him. Sue Beach. He was sure of the bride's name. Or Shirley? He was certain he had the right family but was Sue the mother or the daughter?

The congregation was getting impatient, the bride and groom were eyeing each other, ready to call the whole thing off. Brother Patrick knew he could delay no longer. In his desperation, he whispered a prayer and the answer descended like a dove. He would get the names from the bride and groom. Turning to the groom, he asked, "In what name do you come to be married?"

The groom's eyes rolled back in his head. No one told him that question was going to be on the exam. His agile brain raced through the lecture his mother had given him about honeymoon finances, the speech his father had made about motel etiquette, the Chillicothe high school Fight song, the creed of the Future Farmers of America, back to the summer he went to Vacation Bible School. "I come," he said, "in the name of our Lord Jesus Christ."

In desperation Brother Patrick gave up the game. "What does your mother call you?" he asked.

"Puffen," said Ben Tooley.

"Puffen," Brother Patrick said, "do you take—" The bride's first name had slipped completely from his head. "Do you take this Beach to be your wife?"

The affair was such a disaster that afterwards at every wedding, for as long as Brother Patrick was pastor, the bride and groom wore name tags. There was even a ceremony where the best man got to remove the bride's name tag from her shoulder pad. Men who had married women from outside Chillicothe had to explain the custom. But in Chillicothe the name tags became so popular that some Methodists wore them at their weddings. The Methodists, though, went in more for plastic rather than the traditional mother of pearl.

Weddings were among my favorite times. What were your favorite times?

Joyce: My favorite time was the Depression.

Bob: In Chillicothe we didn't know when the depression began. We didn't know when it was over either.

Joyce: During the Depression, nobody had anything, but we all had such a large share of nothing and we all had nothing in equal proportions. Nobody had more of nothing than any other person had of nothing and so we all had plenty. And when you have plenty, then no one wants for more. My daddy had a job, my mother was my mother and I was an only child. We could hardly keep up with the schedule for the week. There was church twice on Sunday, well, really four times, if you counted Sunday School and Training Union and once Wednesday or twice if you counted Girls Auxiliary or Royal Ambassadors before prayer meeting. There was school every day. Girls Scouts met on Thursday afternoon. UIL practice in softball, or play practice or extemporaneous speaking or poetry reading took up the spring. Football and band when we could field either a team or a band took up the Fall. Ice Cream socials and horseback riding every day filled up the summer unless you broke it up with a camping trip or two to the Brazos River to hunt lunatics. Every other minute was taken up with scripture memorizing or Bible study to help fill in the gaps in our educations.

Sometimes we tried to rest up a little. Mostly we rested in the summer time lying out in the yard on a quilt beneath a highway of Milky Way stars. The full moon gave you a general idea about how far up heaven was, and the dark ground which held my body and those of my playmates marked down as far as any of us thought about going. Outer boundaries changed with whatever mental images we conjured brought on by ghost stories, songs with four part harmony, family sagas, recounting of brave or tender lovers, dirty jokes, word games, how Ruth said "Whither thou goest" and little Samuel said, "Speak for thy servant heareth." I first heard the line, "I have seen the world in a blade of grass" and later knew that I could not see the microcosm in a blade of grass. I did, however, know the world contained on the perfect square of a family mosaic quilt or a courthouse square and knew that latitude and longitude were ample enough to reveal the universe, were at the very least as big as the universe.

My second favorite occasion was World War Two. World War Two only confirmed my good judgment about the Depression. We knew joy collectively and sorrow too. Even our soldiers from Jacksboro went as a group into battle because they were a National Guard unit. Collectively they went overseas and disappeared collectively as a part of the Lost Battalion in the jungles of Burma. And as a town we waited somewhere between life and death, lost and found, anticipation and dread until the Lost should reappear. But we waited together.

I even learned that the world is not square but round in Jacksboro. Down on my knees beside my grandmother as she prayed and I repeated the lines after her, I learned that the world stretched beyond the square and only became rounded with the journey from self. I became acquainted with the Japanese, "those slanty-eyed, runty Japs" who terrorized my Uncle Fred at Iwo Jima or when he found himself penned on the beach in a snow storm dressed in Navy blue winter gear. I learned too of those "boot stomping Hitler-Germans" in Africa with Rommel, the Desert Fox, who thwarted my Uncle Glen, the Odessa Oilfield Giant. And from the same heart's words I learned "forgive seventy times seven"— two lessons at the same time and from the same mouth of a grandmother whose last name was Hartman.

In other ways I learned two lessons which always live side by side in a small town—the best and the worst.

And I learned about triangles. God the father, God the Son and God the Holy Spirit: thesis, antithesis, synthesis; triads, triarchy, triaxial, tricycles. From Jacksboro I early found the Texas triptych—Texas fact, fiction and folklore.

I learned my colors and my shapes; squares, rectangles, triangles, and that one meaning of round is "without sharp edges." Jacksboro taught me all I need to know or ever needed to know. All the lessons came from a sense of place and being appropriate to that time and place no matter how it might look to someone else because you couldn't help yourself.

Maybe it is true that you can't really go home again. But you carry home with you over the years for better or worse. Sometimes home hangs like an albatross around my neck and "with a glittering eye" I must speak of Jacksboro and "all those who dwell therein." At times, I exorcise the pain and sometimes, as if by the telling, I speak the place into existence like Brigadoon. The sense of that place and those people is never very far from my mind and rises both bidden and unbidden to haunt, to comfort, to terrorize and to charm, to find its way into my words both written and spoken.

Bob: The best thing about Chillicothe was everyone was your family. They may not have been your friend but they treated you like family. They spoke when they passed on the street. They waved when they passed on the road. They stopped if you looked like you needed help. And if you were in trouble the whole town was on your side. Wherever I may be in the world, I know that in Chillicothe folks still sing about "A Hill Far Away."

Joyce: My favorite song is "Softly and Tenderly."

Bob: Why?

Joyce: Because it's about home and heaven. I think heaven will surely contain some of Jacksboro and Chillicothe, or I won't go. And when the song says, "Come home, come home; ye who are weary come home" I know The Father had Jacksboro and Chillicothe in mind.

Bob: Bless our towns, bless our homes, and bless all those within them.

Enduring Love ～

Jean and Robert Flynn

Jean Flynn:

We have been told numerous times that our marriage should have failed. We are opposites. We view things differently. Robert is a romantic; I am a realist. When two people are so different, one always has to compromise. I compromised on a wedding anniversary trip.

We gave ourselves a five week trip to Alaska for our fortieth wedding anniversary. Our first adventure was to backpack the Chilkoot Trail, the site of the Klondike Gold Rush. I had envisioned wine by a campfire, the smells of food cooking, and sleeping bags zipped together under the stars.

By the time I had finished packing my thirty-five pound backpack, I had drunk all the wine and we had settled on freeze-dried food. Our fire was a pork'n'beans can over a Sterno. It was June; there was still snow and ice everywhere.

We were both layered with clothes; the outer garment was waterproof— Bob's was Goretex, mine was Wal-Mart. The only things I took off at night were my wet socks and rainsuit. There were no stars because it never got dark and every time I went to sleep, I was startled awake by Bob blowing the bear whistle in my ear.

The third day of our hike, we climbed the Chilkoot Pass, seven miles at a 45 degree angle from the base to the summit. I don't remember how long it took us because it is an outdoor museum. I stopped several times to explore areas scattered with old pans, cans, parts of cooking stoves, and graves.

It was late when we arrived at Happy Camp, an oxymoron if I have ever heard one. It was also snowing. We set up our tent. I took off my wet socks and suit and said, "I'm going to bed. Don't blow the whistle. If a bear comes, let him have me."

As I curled up in the sleeping bag, I silently prayed, "Lord, if you will just let me get dry and warm again, I promise to divorce Robert Flynn before our next anniversary!"

Robert Flynn:

For our fortieth anniversary, I wanted to do something romantic. Alaska! Lying beside a bubbling stream under a clear starry sky with wine in our hands, a campfire at our feet and miles of nothing in every direction. However, when we got to Alaska, Jean wanted to go to Canada. I was willing to compromise; that's what enduring love means. The cheapest way was to climb the Chilkoot Trail. We made the trip to Canada in three days, but perhaps could have beaten the record for married couples who are not pursued by bears if Jean had not stopped so often. She said she wanted to see what the Klondikers had left. Like dead horses.

Jean carried a backpack with a package of M&Ms. I carried the food, the water, the tent, the sleeping bags, Jean's reading material and a bottle of chilled wine. For food, I carried freeze dried MRE's—a four day supply of tuna fish casserole. Following military tradition, the army replaced inedible ham and lima beans with freeze-dried tuna fish casserole.

When we crossed into Canada we found seven feet of snow covering a narrow trail along the side of a mountain. About a hundred feet below the slippery trail was a lake, still frozen over but showing patches of blue where the ice was getting thin. I told Jean not to worry because if she fell I would get out of my clothes and plunge down the mountainside to rescue her from the lake. Jean told me not to bother about coming to get her out. She would freeze to death before I could get out of the backpack.

We celebrated our anniversary at Happy Camp. There were no stars because it was snowing, no campfire because there was no wood, and no wine because Jean drank it the first night. I set up the tent, unrolled the sleeping bags on the snow and Jean crawled into one. I heated chocolate on the Sterno and brought hot chocolate and M&Ms to bed.

I think we both agreed it was the best anniversary ever. We were both quiet for a while but I knew what Jean was thinking— where will we celebrate our forty-first anniversary? Botswana, I thought. Or maybe, Bangladesh.

Lions in Camp —

Dedicated to John Ochieng who died of malaria

The road to Ewaso Ngiro was so rough I bounced off the seat and bumped my head on the roof of the vehicle. It was so rough my wife said the thing she most regretted not bringing to Africa was a jogging bra. But it was going to be worth it. We had left the tourist track, and after half an hour we left the rutted track. This was Masai territory, an area few non-Masai ever saw.

This was not a Kenya game reserve. This was the Ewaso Ngiro Plain, unmarked by roads. Masai herdsmen watched us pass, as did herds of zebra, impala, and wildebeest. We drove across the plain until we reached a riverine acacia forest on the edge of the Loita Hills. The Bantu drivers guided the truck and two vans around acacia, thorn bush, and deep holes left by anteaters, and stopped in a thicket.

Two vultures watched our arrival with veiled interest. Sunlight filtered dimly through the trees. The earth was invisible beneath high grass and low bushes. I looked out the window in disbelief. This couldn't be our campsite; this was jungle.

As a native Texan I had an in-bred suspicion of brush and high grass that could harbor centipedes, scorpions, spiders, and snakes. Most snakes, I knew, were non-poisonous. In Texas. The only non-poisonous snake in Kenya was the python.

When John Ochieng told us to get out, I, like the others, left my belongings inside the vehicle. I wasn't convinced this was going to be our camp until the drivers dumped the tents on the ground and the cooks, armed with machetes, chopped a "kitchen" out of the undergrowth beneath a tree.

Ochieng, who spoke fluent English, Swahili, and several tribal dialects, led us around the campground to put us at ease. He was a teacher, naturalist, and survival instructor, and he gave us En-

51

glish and Swahili names for the birds, trees, and bushes and laughed at our concern for snakes in the high grass. "Go slow and single file," he advised us. "They'll get out of your way. If you crowd up and trap them between you, they'll coil and strike."

I joined the end of the single file as Ochieng led us on a hike to a spring and along the river. Weaver nests hung from the trees. A yellow-billed stork waded in the shallow water. It was a peaceful scene and when we returned, camp didn't seem so hostile. Ochieng pointed out the toilets—men to the left of the tents, women to the right, no one toward the spring, and all tissue paper was to be brought back to camp and burned. Ochieng was also an ecologist.

Under his direction, we set up our tents in a close semi-circle and rolled out our sleeping bags. The tent was of the utilitarian variety. It was high enough that I could crawl in and sit up, long enough that I could stretch out my full six feet, and wide enough for two people or two intimate friends and one duffel bag. It contained the essentials—a fly for deflecting rain, netting for keeping out flies and mosquitoes, a floor to provide separation, if not total protection, from water, scorpions, ants, and snakes, and sides that were impervious to lions. That was what Ochieng assured us. And he was an experienced guide and survival instructor.

Ochieng suffered from a recurrence of malaria, and, after inspecting the location of the tents, he went to sleep, telling us that we could explore the area as long as we did not go alone, told the others where we were going, and kept in the clearings and away from the bush. My wife and I walked out of the forest to explore the plains. Masai cattle kept the grass short, and we avoided the occasional thickets. We saw ring-necked doves, rabbits, and dik-dik. We picked up two skulls and three jawbones and tried to identify the animals they had belonged to. Two Masai wearing red togas and beaded necklaces, and carrying clubs and short stabbing spears, began following us. They shouted, waved, and made gestures which we interpreted as signals warning us away from something, perhaps their herds. We returned to the camp.

Two other Masai, who looked like teenage boys, came to the camp to stare curiously at our pale faces. The Masai, who have little body hair, felt the hair on my forearm. A young woman with shoulder-length brunette hair drew particular attention. They touched her hair and examined it with their fingers. One of the young men had two wives, five children and 150 cattle and was interested in the brunette for a third wife.

The brunette, who was going to be a teaching assistant at Ohio State University in the fall, believed her father would be flattered at the offer of 150 cattle, until one of the drivers explained that the Masai had not offered all his cattle. Negotiation with her father was still to take place. The brunette abandoned the courtship and withdrew to her tent.

After the Masai left, I walked a short distance behind the tents and watched the sun set through the flat-topped thorn trees. The sky went blue, to pink, to orange, to crimson, and the insects and long-tailed hoepoes went quiet.

Before the sky turned to black, I joined the others at the folding tables the cooks had set up in a clearing they had hacked out between our tents and the cook area. John Mbogo, chief cook, brought lentil soup, which was salty but delicious. The soup was always salty but delicious. I had almost finished mine when a lion roared just beyond the cook area. The cooks and drivers reassembled at our table, grabbing our lanterns and pointing flashlights at the bushes on three sides of the kitchen. Mbogo saw a lion beside the truck that carried the food and tents.

It wasn't the presence of the lions that was frightening; it was the fact that the cooks and drivers were scared. They started two roaring bonfires, one near our table and the other near the kitchen. Mbogo had two flashlights in one hand and appropriated mine because it was more powerful.

"We know the lions in the game reserves," he explained. "We know what they'll do. These lions aren't used to people. We don't know what they'll do." He played the flashlight beams on the darkness beyond the dim light of the lanterns.

A lion was in heavy brush, and all we could see was the glitter of his eye, first one eye and then the other as the head moved through the brush. The lion was walking toward us. While Mbogo and I watched the glittering eye, a big lioness walked through the beam of the flashlight. The lioness was twenty yards away, and as soon as she disappeared into the darkness, Mbogo and I backed up to the fire.

We turned for advice to Ochieng, who was drowsing at the table. He assured us that the lions would not come into the camp with all of us yelling and running around, and that lions would not come into the tents. We searched the darkness with our flashlights for several minutes and then gathered around the fire. It took longer for the cooks to return to the cook fire, because the kitchen had brush on three sides. While Mbogo finished dinner, Elijah watched.

Mbogo and Elijah brought fresh salad, sweet and sour pork, and fresh corn and peas to the table, but we were slow to settle down enough to eat. We all wanted to tell what we had seen or heard. Only a few of us had seen the lions, but everyone had heard them. No one was certain how many lions there had been, but Mbogo thought there were two lionesses and some younger lions.

I had scarcely tasted my dessert of fresh fruit cocktail when a lion roared from the bush outside the kitchen. We deserted the table again to look for the lions. I'm not sure why we were looking for the lions, but the cooks and drivers ran from one side of the camp area to the other flashing their lights on the darkness, so we joined them. I think no one wanted to see the lions but everyone wanted to know where they were.

A lion roared on the other side of the camp. They had circled and were now behind our tents. The cooks and drivers threw wood on both fires, and we returned to the table, fetched our chairs, and dragged them to the blaze. We finished dessert and took our coffee or hot chocolate huddled around the fire. The evening was cool but we were huddling more for spiritual than physical comfort.

We sat by the fire, watching our backs and trying to scare each other. Ochieng slept in his chair. He roused from time to time to assure us that lions would not come into tents, and in an act of mercy we insisted that he go to bed, as he had a high fever.

We lingered by the fire, drinking coffee and hot chocolate, listening to the lions that had stilled the other sounds of the night. No one really wanted to go to bed. We enjoyed our coffee, one another's company, and the roaring of the lions. No one wanted to walk to his or her tent alone.

After a time the women organized a trip to the powder room and trooped off together. I watched them leave with some disappointment. My wife was among them, which meant I would walk to the tent alone. After a few jokes about women traveling in herds, we men said goodnight, and manfully walked alone. I talked the whole way to the other men, who were also talking. I wanted everyone to know where I was, and my mouth prepared to scream.

I zipped up the mosquito netting but left the outside covering open so that I could see. I couldn't see the lions, but they got so close Mbogo drove his vehicle behind the tents to drive them away.

I went to sleep and was awakened by the roar of a lion that sounded like it was between our tent and the kitchen. My wife and I got out of our bags to look through the mosquito netting but could see nothing. We could, however, hear the lion padding behind the tent. Then we again heard one of the vehicles start and drive behind the tents. After that, we heard the lions but never again so close.

As early as two o'clock, I regretted the two cups of coffee mocha I had enjoyed in the camaraderie of the campfire. By three o'clock I was in heavy internal debate as to the prudence of leaving the tent. By three-thirty I was envisioning the headlines I would make after being dragged away by a lion while attending nature's call. Was that the way I wanted my life to end, a victim of healthy kidneys? By four o'clock the debate was over, but I didn't go far; with one hand I kept the flashlight beam making a constant, if not steady, 360 degree sweep.

I was up early the next morning, eager to recount the sounds of the night over a cup of coffee. As recompense for waking my wife during the night to ask her to listen for any strangled screams or sounds of a heavy body being dragged through the brush, I promised to bring her a cup of coffee in bed. However, I was the first one up. The cooks and drivers had abandoned their tents and were asleep in the vehicles. Only we tourists had known the security of the tents.

I sat in one of the camp chairs and relished the tranquility of the morning. I revived the fire and thought over the excitement of the night and the adventure of the day to come. And the lions that would return at nightfall. I decided I liked it. I decided I would be disappointed if the lions didn't return. I decided to limit all liquids after four o'clock in the afternoon and no coffee after dinner.

Growing Up

Truth and Beauty ⟶

To be a writer in Texas is to know truth and beauty. A friend and I were standing in the cotton field one day. It was one of those hundred degree north Texas days when the hot wind blows—and the wind always blows—and it always blows either hot or cold. And the only thing there is to move is sand. And the sand moves every time the wind blows. We were leaning on our hoes, and way off in the distance we could see a pickup truck going down a county road and dragging a cloud of dust behind it. We must have stood there, transfixed, for ten or fifteen minutes, just admiring that cloud of dust on the horizon. My friend said, "Ain't that the prettiest thing you ever saw?" It was my introduction to beauty.

My introduction to truth was not so dramatic. My grandmother was born in Vermont in 1842. That was the year the Webster-Ashburton Treaty was signed between the United States and England settling the boundary of Canada west of Lake Superior. She married my grandfather who was an Irish immigrant and followed him to Texas where he helped build the Fort Worth and Denver Railroad. Grandmother bore him three sons, all born at a constantly moving end of the track. Near Chillicothe my grandfather bought a piece of land. A few years later, 1897, he was murdered. Grandmother hung on to that piece of land and she doomed her children to do the same.

Every day both going and coming from the two room country school I attended, I had to cross over the railroad tracks my grandfather helped to lay. And in both directions the tracks ran as far as the eye could see. A few miles to the east and we would have been in an oil field. A few miles west and we would have been on land good for nothing but running cows and chasing jackrabbits. Slowly the truth appeared on the horizon. My grandfather had been tricked into buying the only place in twenty miles that would grow cotton.

The cotton field is one of the great classrooms of life. Put a young man in a cotton field, place a sack on his back or a hoe in his hand and right away his thoughts will turn to truth and beauty. A far-off look will come into his eye. Put a young man in a cotton field and he will take up prayer. "Lord, if you will just get me out of this, I will never again as long as I live look at the women's underwear in the Sears catalog."

It was in the cotton field that I first learned the power of the English language. I had a girl friend who chopped cotton with me. She was called a hoe hand. I know because my mother told me. As I stood there all alone in the cotton field—my girl friend had been sent home because I used the wrong word—it came to me like a flash of light that if the wrong word like hoer had the power to move my mother to such action, just think what using the right word like hoe hand could accomplish.

That was when I first got the notion of being a writer. I knew it wasn't going to be easy. We didn't go in much for writing at the country school I attended. Writing was something that was done by fairies and other New Yorkers. Real men studied penmanship. We made little push-pull lines all over the page. And row after row of spirals. It was called the Palmer Method and was invented during the Spanish Inquisition as a means of turning boys from writers to pray-ers. "Lord, if you will just get me out of this I will never touch another pencil. And I will never again drop my eraser and try to look up Myrtle Bailey's dress."

But we knew what a writer was. A writer was somebody who was dead. And if he was any good he had been dead a long time. If he was real good, people killed him. They killed him with hemlock. Hemlock was the Greek word for Freshman Composition.

The country school I attended was closed and we were bused to Chillicothe. Chillicothe had a teacher who had seen England. From a boat. She had discovered truth and beauty from eight miles offshore and had come to Chillicothe to share her vision with picturesque rustics. With some timidity I confessed that I too hankered after truth and beauty.

Chillicothe is small. Chillicothe is so small there's only one Baptist Church. Chillicothe is so small you have to go to Quanah to have a coincidence. For a good coincidence you have to go to Vernon. Chillicothe was fairly bursting with truth and beauty and my teacher encouraged me to write about it.

I decided to write about my father. My father, the youngest of three sons, was born in a box car at the end of the track that has since come to be called Chillicothe, Texas, being the first child born in my home town. The box car served as the station house for the railroad, and was, with the exception of a dugout that served as a store, the only building in town. I wrote that my father was born in the finest house in Chillicothe. My teacher told me to write something that had an epiphany. For an epiphany you had to go all the way to Wichita Falls.

I wrote about Delmer Lance's pet heifer, Snuggles. Snuggles was raised on a bottle and was as friendly as you'd want a heifer to be. Until Delmer locked her in the barn with his range bull. The next morning, Snuggles was gone. Also the barn door. The top rail off the fence.

Delmer chased that cow all over the county but Snuggles went wild as a new rope. One night Delmer was driving down the highway and ran over Snuggles. Delmer said he recognized her when she passed over the windshield by the puzzled look on her face. That was an epiphany. I spent half my life thinking I could recognize a bad girl by the puzzled look on her face.

My teacher said to write about something that had happened to me. I wrote about the year there was a blizzard and everybody from the two room country school—two teachers, thirty-eight pupils, and three adults who had sought refuge in the school—had to walk two miles through the snow to our house to spend the night. I remembered it because that was the day my father came home with four hundred baby chickens and it was so cold we had to keep them in the house. All over the house it was butts and feathers. All night it was cheep and shit. Cheep and shit.

Forty-two chickens were squashed in the linoleum. Three drowned in the chamber pot. One was crushed when Ed Byars put on his boots. When Mother lighted the gas oven thirteen went up like a torch. Three more were scorched so bad that Dad threw them out in the snow. Ed Byars spent the rest of his life minus the end of his nose because he preferred frost bite to the smell of singed chicken feathers.

My teacher said I didn't know the first thing about truth or beauty. I promised to go to England the first chance I got. Or at least Korea. She loaned me books that were not available in the Wilbarger County Library, books that had been written by real writers.

Real writers wrote about such things as I had never heard of. Damsels. Splendor falling on castle walls. For splendor we had to go to the Fort Worth Fat Stock Show. Since I wasn't overly familiar with damsels and splendor, I tried reading what real writers wrote about rural life. "Dear child of nature, let them rail. There is a nest in a green vale." Which was pretty mystifying to me. I remember asking Bubba Spivey, "Don't writers get chiggers like everybody else?"

I set out looking for a green vale to make a nest in and when I got there I found out what made it so green. When it comes to vales, a cow will get ahead of you every time.

I wrote a story that contained the wisdom of the world in eight poetic pages of arcane words and mysterious imagery full of towers, turrets, and spires. My teacher loved it. She had never met a symbol she didn't like.

Assured of success, I went to college to become a writer. I knew what I wanted. I wanted to reveal the false hopes, the futile dreams, the fleeting victories, the glorious visions, the hidden desires, the sudden and secret joys, that bind us into one humanity. I wanted to refine the language, to explore the avenues of communication, to stretch the limits of understanding, to probe the mysteries and futilities and glories of man, to heal his broken spirit, to restore his sense of purpose, to discover the nature of beauty and truth, and to sell it to the movies for a million dollars. After which I intended to marry a movie star and move to Paris. Or at least, Commerce.

My instructor told me the way to find truth and beauty was to write about heroes and villains, good people versus bad people. The best people I knew did bad things. The worst people I knew did good things. We weren't heroes or villains, we were just puzzled. How could I write about the people I knew when I was attending a college that did not approve of dancing. Smoking. Swearing. Drinking. Dating members of the opposite sex. Dating members of the same sex. I used to pray, "Lord, if you will just get me out of college I will never be a Christian again."

We were told to write a love story containing truth and beauty. I was petrified. I had never seen a moat or a moor. I had never known a knight or a knave. I was the only great lover I knew. The only time I came close I began nuzzling the girl's ear and lost my chewing gum in her hair. It was Bazooka bubble gum and I hadn't gotten all the sweet out of it. I spent the next hour and forty-five minutes alternating between kissing her eyes and frisking her scalp, and holding my hands over her eyes while chewing her hair. Her mother called her three times before my jaws came unstuck.

I wrote about a boy and a girl. He is true. She is innocent. They have found a nest in a green glade. They smoke a Salem. They speak of truth and beauty.

I threw the story away. I wrote about a boy and a girl. The boy is generally true. The girl is relatively innocent. They find a meadow. The sun is hot, the wind roughens their complexion. They smell of sweat and Salem cigarettes. He speaks of love with some truth. She has a puzzled look on her face.

I tore up the pages. A boy and a girl. He is a bastard. She is a bitch. They are lying in a pasture among cow dung. Scratching chigger bites. The blazing sun raises blisters on his back. He has a herpes on his lip. She has bologna breath. He whispers obscenities into her ear. He loses his gum in her hair. It is Bazooka Bubble Gum and still has some of the sweet in it. Her mother calls. He gnashes his teeth.

I wrote about Bud Tabor. Bud was a married man, and Sherry McIlroy's father shot him through Box 287. Ed McIlroy was the postmaster and when Bud came in to get his mail, Ed stuck a pistol in the open end of the box and shot Bud in the eye. Ed was a conscientious man and he waited until Bud opened the box and looked inside so as not to deface government property.

They never found Bud Tabor's eye. Buried him without it. They fixed him up with a glass eye for the funeral, but Sherry and Bud's wife got in an argument over who got to keep it as a souvenir. Sherry won. Put it on a chain and wore it hanging down between her breasts. Folks used to say Bud may have gone to hell but his eye went to heaven. Some folks idea of heaven is mighty small. Lower on one side than the other.

My instructor said it was not a love story.

Delmer Lance had some sheep but they developed an unnatural affection for an old yellow dog. They followed the dog wherever it went. No pen could hold them for long, and once on his trail, the dog couldn't shake them. In desperation the dog ran away from home, the sheep right behind him.

From time to time the dog and sheep showed up at someone's tank or feed trough, the dog looking gaunt and haunty-eyed, the sheep looking all unraveled. Elmer Spruill shot the dog. Elmer said he couldn't stand the puzzled look in the dog's eyes.

My instructor said there was no beauty, no truth, and no moral.

Lowell Byars came to the county with his wife Lou. They lived in a dugout and poor-boyed, working as long as there was light to see. There was no time for visiting neighbors, or going to church, just day after day of chopping weeds and carrying water, with nothing to eat but biscuits and gravy, and nothing to sleep on but the gritty quilts Lou's mother had given them.

The roof of the dugout caved in during a rain storm, they were dispossessed for two days by a skunk, the crops blew away in a sandstorm, but Lou stuck it out, and if she cried of loneliness or despair it was when Lowell was away from the dugout. One morning Lowell got up early as usual and said, "Get dressed, Lou, we're going to Quanah to see the Mollie Bailey show."

Lowell milked the cow, fed the mules, hitched the wagon, and when he got back to the dugout he had to fix breakfast. Lou was still brushing her hair. They drove to Quanah and watched the wagons come in, drawn by elephants. They looked in the store windows and stared at the crowd of people in town. They drank lemonade and had a supper of sardines and crackers and saw the show and it was over, time to get in the wagon and start for home.

It was a long way back to the dugout and Lowell knew he would have to get up early the next morning to make up for the work he had missed but he didn't care. The moon was bright, a thousand stars twinkled in the sky, and he had shown his wife a sight. Lowell was feeling pleased with himself.

"It ain't so terrible being married to me is it?" he asked Lou who was sitting silent and sleepless beside him. Lou began to cry. She cried all the way home. She cried all night. When he got up the next morning she stopped crying to fix his breakfast, but she wouldn't speak to him for three more days until he cut his hand heading red top maize and she had to ask how he was.

Lowell promised to take her to the Christmas dance and rather than disappoint her they drove fifteen miles in an open wagon in the face of a norther. Lou danced every set of the all night dance. She went home with a fever, took pneumonia, and died of frivolity.

I had found a story with a moral but I also found it wasn't easy writing about people I knew. I got all puzzled. I didn't know what was beautiful, and what was foolish, and where truth lay. Was Lou Byars a silly girl unsuited for a rugged country? Was she the innocent victim of a foolish dream? Or was she a tragic heroine who knew that the quality of life was not measured by the years endured in twilight, but by the moments spent in the candle's flame?

Ideas are so neat. You can outline an idea. You can label an idea. Ideas don't bleed. They don't cry. They don't blame you for their unhappiness. They don't die of frivolity. But a person has many faces. And some of them are evil, and some are vain, and some are foolish, and some are beautiful, and many are secret.

It looked like for truth and beauty you had to cross Red River. All I knew about was a little place called Chillicothe. And it wasn't even the Chillicothe that was on the map. It was a little place I called Wanderer Springs, that existed only in my mind. And all I had to go by was my grandmother who died at the age of ninety the year I was born, and my father who was born in a boxcar at the end of the track. Would truth and beauty as I wrote it stand up against the reality of my grandmother? Would my father believe it? And could it happen within the territory I had staked out for myself?

I wrote the love story of Grover and Edna Turrill. When he was sixteen Grover had married Edna, at the request of both families. Grover's father gave them a milk cow, and Edna's father gave them a steer. Grover yoked them together and started to California. It was his promise to Edna.

They crossed Red River and stopped near Preston where Edna had a baby boy with no one to help her but Grover. They started again as soon as she was able to travel, Edna and the baby in the wagon, and Grover walking beside the wagon, prodding the steer and milk cow, and picking up firewood.

One day Edna placed the sleeping baby in the back of the wagon and got out to walk beside the cow. Grover found a tree stump and not knowing the baby was in the back of the wagon, he threw in the stump, killing his child. Some cowboys found them, two teenagers traveling across the prairie with a dead baby wrapped in a quilt. The cowboys buried the child.

Grover and Edna were still on their way to California when the milk cow died near Wanderer Springs. They lived in the wagon while Grover broke the land with the steer and planted a crop. Later they built a house and had two more children. When Billo was twelve he went hunting on Wanderer Creek with some older boys. They ran a coon up a dead tree, and Billo was sent up the tree to shake the coon down. A pile of brush had been washed up under the tree and the older boys set it afire so that Billo could see. The dead tree caught fire and Billo was burned so he couldn't lie down and Edna and Grover took turns holding him the four days it took him to die.

A few years later, when Polly was thirteen, she complained of a stomach ache. Polly wasn't fat but, like Edna, she was slope-shouldered, solid, and a good eater. When she was unable to eat breakfast, Grover hitched up the wagon, made a pallet in the back, and with Edna to comfort Polly, they started for the doctor in Wanderer Springs, several miles away. The wagon had no springs, the road was just a set of ruts across the prairie, and Polly whimpered the whole way although Grover drove as slowly as he dared.

When they got to Wanderer Springs, they found that Dr. Vestal had been called out of town. Over near Medicine Hill folks thought, expected to be gone all day. Polly was too sick to wait so they started for Medicine Hill, sending word ahead by Buster Bryant who volunteered to carry the message.

It was August and the sun was hot and Polly cried out at every bump, so Edna stood and held a quilt to shade her, and Grover drove the mules as fast as he dared. They met Buster Bryant who had missed Dr. Vestal somehow. The doctor was on his way to Bull Valley. Grover turned the mules toward Bull Valley with Buster racing ahead.

Dr. Vestal had left Bull Valley for Red Top. Buster rode to head off the Turrills. The mules had played out and Grover was walking beside them to lighten the load. Edna was standing with her feet spread, holding the solid little girl in her arms, trying to absorb the bumps and shocks of the wagon with her own body. Buster told them to go home. He would find Dr. Vestal and meet them there.

It was almost dark when the wagon got back home and Buster and the doctor were waiting. Edna was sitting beside Grover holding Polly who was so big she lay across both their laps. The mules stopped of their own accord and neither Grover nor Edna made a move to get down. Dr. Vestal started to the wagon but Grover said, "I don't want you to touch her. We've been praying for you all day and listening to her die. I know it ain't your fault, but I don't want to see you now."

Buster stayed with the Turrills although he didn't dare go in the house. He unhitched the mules and fed them and sat out on the porch. After a while Grover came out. He sat on the porch and stared at the dark, empty, treeless miles over which he had ridden that day, listening to the shriek of the wagon wheels and the dying cries of his last child.

After a while Edna came out also and leaned against the porch post, hugging the porch post as though it were a child, her head hanging down a little as though permanently bent from ironing clothes and chopping cotton. She waited while the last light of day faded and one by one the stars came out, watching the prairie that under moonlight had a sheen like a silent sea.

"If that cow hadn't died, we'd be in California," Grover said.

"Old Boss," Edna said, remembering the name over all the years, recalling the dreams they had shared as they traveled across the prairie in the wagon.

"God damn country," Grover said. "Washes away ever time it rains. Blows away ever time there's a wind. Hail or grasshoppers ever God damn year. Hot as hell or cold as hell. Flood or drought. Too dry to plant to too wet to plow —"

"Yeah," Edna said, nodding her head in the darkness. "But ain't it purty."

Truth in the mythical kingdom of Wanderer Springs was neither comic nor tragic, neither big nor eternal. And it was revealed through the lives of common folk who belched and fornicated, and knew moments of courage, and saw beauty in their meager lives.

But Grover Turrill gave me some problems. Some readers thought the vocabulary was offensive. I could not write about the people I knew without using the vocabulary they knew. My father did not believe a cowboy said "golly bum" when a horse ran him through a bob wire fence.

I went to see Clifford Huff. Clifford was a horseshoer and he had been kicked, bitten, or stepped on by every horse in the county. It gave him an extensive vocabulary. I asked Clifford the worst words he knew. He said they were "yes and no." He had said yes when his wife, Letty, asked him if he was playing around and he had said no when she asked him if the gun was loaded.

They had been married thirty-three years when Letty shot him once through the pantry and twice up the stairs.

Words are not casual things. They are powerful. Even explosive. Words can start wars, or families. Words can wound, they can shock and offend. Words can also heal, and explain, and give hope and understanding. Words have an intrinsic worth, and there is pride and delight in using the right word. Anyone who chops cotton with an axe is a hoer.

I don't know whether or not Travis drew a line at the Alamo. Maybe that story is myth. I do know that every writer draws the line. Must draw the line. Whether he is dealing with teachers, advisors, well-wishers, editors, publishers, critics, or the public. This is my kingdom. These are my people. I know them better than anybody. They will not jump through hoops for the amusement of casual readers. They will not temper their speech for prudish ears. I may not respond the way they do, but I respect them for what they are. And that's where I draw the line.

I wrote a book about people my grandmother would have spoken to, and they used words my father would have believed. A few people heard of it. Fewer read it. My closest friends bought it. And loaned it out. After a while the book disappeared from bookstores to make room for a best seller written by a man who had never met an adverb he didn't like. It was about a lonely but beautiful housewife who falls in love with a handsome painter who is painting the windmills of Concho County for Aquatic Monthly. After three days of romantic bliss, she decides she must be true to her ironing board and he must move on to paint the fence posts of Val Verde.

But I had already turned down the next row. Writing is a lot like chopping cotton. It's a long way to the end of the row, and when you get there, there's always another row to turn down. A friend was disturbed that I was spending so much time at something so unrewarding. "There's no money in it," he said. I couldn't argue with that. There's more fame in selling used cars. There's more fun in running a gas pump. I didn't argue with him because he was right.

I just kept chopping on down the row, knowing when I got to the end of it, there would be another row to turn down. And another. And another. And as the day wore on it wouldn't get any easier. Maybe it wouldn't get any better. Perhaps no one would come out to the field to see if I was still working. I might not even hear the dinner bell. It didn't matter. He thought I was a hoer. But I am a hoe hand.

Jeremiah was a Bulldog ～

As I child I didn't read comic books. They were available but they were pale compared to the stories from the Bible. The best stories were in the Jewish Bible we called the Old Testament. David and Goliath. Samson killing Philistines with the jawbone of an ass. There was nothing in comic books that could match the story of a Levite and his concubine who spent a night in Gibeah.

I read those stories from the authentic King James Baptist Bible that proved that God and Shakespeare spoke the same language. In fact, God sounded a lot like Shakespeare. And so did Jeremiah and Jesus. No one else, except a couple of Marine drill sergeants, came close to sounding like God.

The King James Bible is still my favorite translation to read if I don't have to understand it or read it aloud. I hear echoes of King James in Patrick Henry's "liberty or death" speech, William Butler Travis's last message from the Alamo "to the People of Texas and All Americans in The World," Lincoln's Gettysburg Address, Martin Luther King's "I have a dream." They couldn't match the signification of God, but real men always sound a little profuse when they speak.

My childhood heroes were from that Bible: Abraham, Isaac, Joseph, King David, Samson, Sam Houston, Robert E. Lee, Stonewall Jackson. Well, some of those weren't from the Bible but it took me a while to separate them.

Few Texas children of my day would have been surprised to discover that the heroes of the Jewish Bible had been Texans. They seemed peculiarly Texan, although perhaps born in Tennessee or Virginia. Maybe it was their outsized virtues and vices. The Hebrew kings could have used some generals like Sam Houston, Robert E. Lee, Nathan Bedford Forrest or Stonewall Jackson.

James Bowie, William Butler Travis and Davy Crockett would have been at home during the sieges of Jerusalem but probably would have chosen different deaths at Masada.

The patriarchs, judges, prophets, even the kings of the Jewish Bible seemed Texan, or at least southern. They were our heroes, our history, our mythology, almost our family. They were close to our lives. Rural folks, a lot of them, shepherds, cattle owners. My father was what was genteelly known as a farmer-stockman. We raised crops and livestock. Some days I worked in the field and some days I worked with animals. How could I not identify with Hebrew heroes? How could not any southern boy? I herded sheep and cattle and saw myself as an ancient Hebrew writing psalms. I worked the fields with one eye searching the horizon for Philistines. Like the Hebrews we were surrounded by trouble but overshadowed by a watchful, if demanding, God.

Adam and Eve, with Eve getting the blame for everything, was a southern story. Cain and Abel was certainly a southern story, although I think most southern folks preferred Cain. The feuding of Isaac and Ishmael was as serious and long-lasting as any southern feud. The sibling rivalry between Jacob and Esau was something that I and most southern boys understood in our bones, although I suspect most of us preferred Esau. Jacob was too much a Yankee trader. God does not always pick the right side. Joseph and King David could have been charismatic southern politicians with the kind of devoted followers that Robert E. Lee had and Lincoln didn't.

Samson and Delilah was the quintessential southern story. The strong, soft-hearted and weak-willed hero pitted against the delicate but steely flower of southern maidenhood who wins first his heart and then his head.

King Saul was a southern story. Saul was almost a Jefferson Davis. The tall, humorless, egoistic, deluded hero promoted to power he was unable to harness, who understood neither God nor His people, neither the present nor the future. I saw a tragic grandeur in King Saul watching a virile young man upstaging him, a songster who, as yet, knew nothing of defeat and despair.

No matter if Saul killed a thousand, David killed ten thousand. No matter if Lee killed a thousand, Grant had ten thousand more.

An old order was ending, a new one beginning: a major theme in Southern literature. Saul's meeting with the witch of Endor, seeking his departed glory in the spirit of the dead prophet Samuel, reverberated in Nathan Bedford Forrest pledging as Grand Wizard of the Ku Klux Klan to protect southern whites from indignities and to defend the constitution of the United States.

Southerners read Israel's and/or Judah's history as our own. Ministers, and sometimes teachers, compared the South to fallen Israel that would be redeemed. We were God's chosen people. Our forefathers had fought a holy war and had lost because God was punishing us for our sins. (Slavery and racism were not among them.)

Southern boys, even those on frontiers like West Texas, breathed the glories of the Lost Cause and the noble giants who fought not for slavery but for principle, for honor, for home. The North had been driven mad with liberty, when what was needed was authority. The Confederacy was the emblem of virtue, morality and religious principle. Never mind that my paternal grandparents were from the North. That was probably true of half those in my hometown. The Noble South was a concept, an ideal, a myth that rarely collided with reality.

I attended the burial of my maternal great-grandfather, a Confederate veteran. My childhood, and that of many other southern children, was touched by fallen heroes beset by demons, clinging to the tattered remains of their glory, their chivalric code of Christian virtue and military honor. As one Confederate veteran wrote for his epitaph, "An unreconstructed Johnnie, who never repented, who fought for what he knew to be right from '61 to '65 and received one Mexican dollar for two years' service. Belonged to the Ku Klux Klan, a deacon in the Baptist Church and a Master Mason for forty years." That man could have been in Jerusalem throwing stones at Jeremiah.

Jeremiah was the true southern hero. Jeremiah tried to save Jerusalem from Babylon but failed. Jeremiah could have been under siege in Atlanta with Sherman's troops ravaging the countryside, or maybe even in the Alamo.

The book of Jeremiah begins like a southern story. "Did you hear what Jeremiah said, Hilkiah's boy? those folks from Anathoth? Benjamin county?" The upward inflection not directed at the reader's doubt but her memory. "You know, old Jeremiah from over Anathoth way."

Jeremiah sounds like a southern boy. "Before I formed thee in the belly I knew thee; and before thou camest forth out of the womb I sanctified thee, and I ordained thee a prophet unto the nations." (Jeremiah 1:5) And Jeremiah said, "Who me? You talking to me? I'm just a kid. I'm not one of them rarified folks. Well, okay, if you're sure you want me to."

Jeremiah even preached the kinds of sermons I heard almost every Sunday, in almost the same language. "Wherefore I will yet plead with you, saith the Lord, and with your children's children will I plead. For pass over the isles of Chittim and see; and send unto Kedar and consider diligently, and see if there be such a thing. Hath a nation changed their gods, which are yet no gods? but my people have changed their glory for that which doth not profit. Be astonished, O ye heavens, at this, and be horribly afraid, be ye very desolate, saith the Lord. For my people have committed two evils; they have forsaken me the fountain of living waters, and hewed them out cisterns, broken cisterns, that can hold no water." (Jeremiah 2:9-13)

We heard the prophets' cries for a return to the living waters of the past as moral guides for our own land. In my youth, in country churches in the south, preachers still advocated the virtues of the Confederacy: a hierarchical social order just as in heaven, a benevolent paternalism of man over woman, minister over church, white over black and non-European immigrants, and God over all; and a moralistic, non-materialistic society. That nobility was being abandoned, preachers said, and we children were embracing the commerce and materialism of the evil North that had introduced its false god Mammon in our conquered but holy land.

We southerners were heirs to an unquestioned moral superiority but my generation was in danger of abandoning the true moral standard to lust after materialism and worldliness. Sermons were illustrated with stories of Robert E. Lee who chose to be a poorly paid educator rather than seeking financial or political gain from the glorious sacrifices of his men. Ministers compared Lee's temptations to Christ's temptations; Lee rejected money, power and fame to fight for right. "Simplicity, hardihood, self-sacrifice," our preachers thundered. General Kirby Smith died deeply in debt shortly after rejecting a financial offer to lend his name to a lottery. "Better to be ennobled by poverty," we were taught, "than to be corrupted by Yankees and their gold."

Preachers also preached against other uniquely Northern sins imposed on a demoralized and impoverished people. Demon Rum, distilled in the North to corrupt the South. Preachers quoted our saint, Stonewall Jackson. "I am more afraid of King Alcohol than of all the bullets of the enemy." My friends and I eschewed alcohol in our make-believe battles where we sank bayonets in Sherman, and especially that sot, Ulysses Grant.

Carpetbaggers had sneaked gambling into the poverty-ridden South, but it would be sin to gamble in the land of men of honor and integrity like Robert E. Lee and Stonewall Jackson. Wealth was to be feared, if not despised. Southerners did not flaunt wealth, they quietly used it in the service of God and in open-hearted hospitality. That hospitality did not extend to former slaves or immigrants with foreign religions that Yankees had thrust upon us. "The south above any other section represents Anglo-Saxon, native-born America," claimed Episcopal Bishop Theodore DuBose Bratton. "The preservation of the American government is in the hands of the South, because Southern blood is purely American." The Philistines lived among us but mostly they lived in the evil cities and worked in factories, enslaved by the lust of the eye.

There was something else that made Jeremiah especially appealing to me. Jeremiah was a failure, and I had certainly failed at everything that mattered. I wanted to be a star on the football field and I was almost never on the field, barely on the team. I wanted to be a star so I could be humble. You can't be humble if you're not a star; you're just someone who has nothing to be proud of.

I was a cavalier student, with a splendid disdain for the grubby competition for grades. The girl I really liked preferred a boy who cussed when I had given up cussing and chewing tobacco so God would be on my side. God has never had much luck with women.

Jeremiah was also extremely unpopular. I wasn't extremely unpopular or even unpopular. I was elected class president one year, and class favorite, and one year I was runner-up for Sweetheart of the Future Homemakers of America, local branch. I just wasn't as popular as I wanted to be, as popular as my charm and good looks deserved, and I liked to imagine it was because I, like Jeremiah, was set apart to be unloved by God's call. There was something romantic about being disliked because one was especially truthful, noble, faithful and forthright.

There was another reason that I was drawn to Jeremiah, a reason I didn't tell anyone. I wanted to write the words that would save my country, that would mend its ways, heal its spirit and make it grand and noble the way it, or at least the Confederacy, had once been. To do that, I needed credentials. No one listened to me. I needed God to validate me so folks would recognize that I was born in the castle, that I was authentic, that I had something to say.

God failed me, just as he failed Jeremiah. Jeremiah was unable to establish the authenticity of his voice. The rulers and the people preferred the prophets who made happy talk and cried "peace" when there was no peace. "A wonderful and horrible thing is committed in the land; the prophets prophesy falsely, and the priests bear rule by their means; and my people love to have it so: and what will ye do in the end thereof?" (Jeremiah 5:30,31)

Jeremiah was commanded not to have a wife and family as a living metaphor and warning of the destruction to come. He was censored by the king, who threw Jeremiah's book in the fire. He was mocked, called a traitor and thrown into a cistern to die.

God's words were such a burden that Jeremiah wanted to stop prophesying.

"O Lord, thou hast deceived me, and I was deceived: thou art stronger than I, and hast prevailed: I am in derision daily, every one mocketh me. For since I spake, I cried out, I cried violence and spoil; because the word of the Lord was made a reproach unto me, and a derision, daily. Then I said, I will not make mention of him, nor speak any more in his name. But his word was in mine heart as a burning fire shut up in my bones, and I was weary with forbearing, and I could not stay." (Jeremiah 20: 7-9)

I thought I could handle the scorn that went with an unpopular message, the frustration of not being heard, of being misunderstood, of being censored. Maybe even being thrown into a cistern. But I could already tell that not having a wife was going to be a problem.

In time I realized that Jeremiah wasn't a Southern hero after all. The South had no Jeremiah. "For among my people are found wicked men: they lay wait, as he that setteth snares; they set a trap, they catch men. As a cage is full of birds, so are their houses full of deceit: therefore they are become great, and waxen rich. They are waxen fat, they shine: yea, they overpass the deeds of the wicked: they judge not the cause, the cause of the fatherless, yet they prosper; and the right of the needy do they not judge. Shall I not visit for these things? saith the Lord: shall not my soul be avenged on such a nation as this?" (Jeremiah 5:26-29)

Sam Houston preached against the evil of secession. Sam, not notoriously pious, lost all the credit he had earned at San Jacinto and as First President of the Republic of Texas supporting the union. If it hadn't been for San Jacinto, he very well might have been hanged by less heroic southerners.

And from those who were supposed to be the moral and spiritual leaders? Not silence; that might have been understood. Methodists, Baptists and Presbyterians in the south seceded from their Northern brethren even before the states did in order to begin the creation of a civil religion that defended slavery by citing Biblical examples of it and interpreting a passage in Genesis to doom blacks to eternal servitude. There was no judgment of slavery and racism by the Christian love ethic. No one recalled the words of Jeremiah: "Woe unto him that buildeth his house by unrighteousness, and his chambers by wrong; that useth his neighbor's service without wages, and giveth him not for his work . . ." (Jeremiah 22:13)

Southern culture, they preached, was the high-water mark of civilization and Northern industrialization was sinful and inhumane. The Southern cause was a holy one, and when the war began, battle victories were seen as God's blessing. Defeats were God's punishment for sin. G.W. Anderson wrote, "As the Israelites at every stop were wont to set up the tabernacle and offer sacrifices to the God of battles, so at every stop Confederates would arrange at once for religious worship—their sacrifices the souls of brave men, who might fall in battle the next day, offering themselves to God by faith." The war was a baptism of blood through which the Confederacy would find redemption.

No one cried, "Therefore thus saith the Lord; Ye have not hearkened unto me, in proclaiming liberty, every one to his brother, and every man to his neighbor: behold, I proclaim a liberty for you, saith the Lord, to the sword, to the pestilence and to the famine..." (Jeremiah 34: 17)

Identifying the South as God's chosen people left little room for self-criticism. Defeat in war and occupation by enemy troops did not threaten that self-identity but strengthened the South's identification with fallen Israel. After the war, religious and moral leaders did not attack the evils of southern culture that had led to defeat. In ensuing years they did not attack white supremacy, the oppression of labor, of the weak and the poor. They did not demand rights for women, blacks and other minorities. They sought to preserve the status quo using the defeated warriors as saints in the civil religion.

The South was devoid of a Jeremiah until Martin Luther King called us out of our slavery to the false god, the Golden Confederacy. When his voice was stilled, a thousand other voices took up the cry. "Return, thou backsliding Israel, saith the Lord; and I will not cause mine anger to fall upon you: for I am merciful, saith the Lord, and I will not keep anger for ever." (Jeremiah 3:12)

After I spent some time in the Marines I began to see Jeremiah in a new light. Southern Christianity closely linked military and religious values. The romantic South loved the cavalier, Robert E. Lee. The moralistic South identified with the puritan, Stonewall Jackson. They were both role models of Christian manhood.

Sometimes, it seemed to me the Confederates had won the war. The Southern ideal of rugged individualism for white men and family values for blacks, women and other unfortunates had swept the land. Military honor and Christian virtue, or at least Judeo/Christian virtue, dominated America. Spiritual leaders from the North joined their Southern brethren in singing praises for military and economic aggrandizement. Episcopal minister and Confederate veteran Randolph McKim saw World War One as "a Crusade. The greatest in history—the holiest. It is in the profoundest sense a Holy War." He saw little room for debate about the issue. "If the pacifists' theory be correct how could Robert E. Lee have been such a saint as he was?"

To be an American Christian male, especially a good American Christian male, one had to serve in his country's military. I enlisted in the Marines during Korea, seeing it as much a religious as a military duty. Thousands of others from all over the country raced to the flag and cross during Vietnam, Desert Storm and briefer, lesser wars to make sacrifice to Mammon and to Mars. The American military-industrial complex had become the religious-military-industrial complex.

Today Americans are obsessed with celebrity, popularity, being loved, being successful. We have difficulty identifying with Jeremiah who was a failure, a pariah. We are flag-waving patriots, quick to ascribe God's name to commercial, political, military adventuring. Jeremiah was not loyal to civil or religious authority. He condemned priests and prophets whose loyalty was to the crown rather than to the truth. Like other prophets, Jeremiah compared Israel's apostasy to adultery and described her as "A wild ass used to the wilderness, that snuffeth up the wind at her pleasure; in her occasion who can turn her away? all they that seek her will not weary themselves; in her month they shall find her." (Jeremiah 2:24)

He was branded a traitor and was beaten and imprisoned. Political leaders called for his death because he demoralized the people in time of war.

"Therefore the princes said unto the king, We beseech thee, let this man be put to death: for thus he weakneneth the hands of the men of war that remain in this city, and the hands of all the people, in speaking such words unto them: for this man seeketh not the welfare of this people, but the hurt." (Jeremiah :38:4) That has a contemporary ring to it, doesn't it?

Despite his faithfulness to the truth, the siege of Jerusalem was temporarily lifted and Jeremiah was mocked and the false prophets were celebrated for their pleasing words. Despite the wrong-headedness of his people, Jeremiah remained in the city to share their fate. He wept over the destruction to come, and while the beloved city burned, the destroyer, Nebuchadnezzar, offered Jeremiah a reward for his usefulness to the enemy. Jeremiah, who had tried to save Jerusalem. Imagine Jeb Stuart being offered a medal by Lincoln for his service to the Union.

Jeremiah remained with his people, and when they fled to Egypt he went with them, and was appalled at how quickly they embraced heathen gods. After that, Jeremiah is lost in the mist of tradition, but certainly he died as unloved and as unpopular as he lived. Despite the tragedy and despair in his own life and in all he saw around him, Jeremiah proclaimed hope. "But this shall be the covenant that I will make with the house of Israel; After those days, saith the Lord, I will put my law in their inward parts, and write it in their hearts; and will be their God, that they shall be my people. And they shall teach no more every man his neighbor, and every man his brother saying, Know the Lord: for they shall all know me, from the least of them unto the greatest of them, saith the Lord: for I will forgive their iniquity, and I will remember their sin no more." (Jeremiah 31: 33,34)

I didn't have a childhood hero from what we called the New Testament. I preferred the Jewish Bible, that was also my Bible. The stories were better. The New Testament had nothing to compare with Shadrach, Meshach and Abednego in the fiery furnace, Daniel in a den of lions, Samson killing a lion, David killing Goliath and a lot of other people. Feeding five thousand wasn't nearly as interesting. Feeding the hungry has never been as much fun as slaying the wicked. Not as rewarding either.

Where were the stories of fathers and sons? Of Abraham offering Isaac to God? Of Isaac blessing Jacob rather than his favorite, Esau. David weeping for Absalom. Jesus told stories about a father welcoming a prodigal son and a father having two sons, one who says he will obey but doesn't and one who says he won't but does. Preachers and Sunday School teachers pointed out that the father in the parables was God, not a human parent.

Where were the stories of friendship closer than brothers such as David and Jonathan? Where were the stories of sibling rivalry such as Cain and Abel? Jacob and Esau? Joseph and his brothers who sold him into slavery? Jesus' disciples John and James, and Peter and Andrew did seek to be the greatest in the new kingdom, but they competed as much with the other disciples as with their brothers.

As I mentioned before, I didn't like the idea of Jeremiah not getting married. That seemed altogether too much just to make a point; but where were the great love stories in the New Testament? Jesus spoke of two bodies becoming one flesh in a mystical union. Ministers, when they spoke of sex at all, spoke of it as communion. I had dimly recognized sex as the articulation of the sacred and profane, the spiritual and the temporal, the love of God and the love of woman, the intimacy of religious worship and the intimacy of physical adoration. I didn't know how, but I wanted to find out.

I needed answers about love and sex and I didn't want to learn from schoolmates who were as puzzled as I was, or ministers who didn't think much about it, or from my parents who didn't know much about it. I sought insight into life where I had always sought it—in stories. Particularly Bible stories, such as Samson and Delilah, Abraham and Sarah, Isaac and Rebekah, Jacob waiting fourteen years for Rachel, Joseph fleeing Potiphar's wife, Samson pursuing Delilah, David seeing Bathsheba at her bath, Solomon and his thousand wives and concubines. Where were the great love stories of the New Testament? There was Jesus, but Jesus loved everyone, even more than Solomon loved.

Jesus said two bodies could become one flesh. Where were the examples? Jesus was an example of perfection and he never thought about sex. Judas was an example of failure and he didn't seem to think about sex either. Peter was bumbling enough to be a reasonable role model and he was married, too. He had a mother-in-law and perhaps children. However, the Christian writers give us no scenes of Peter explaining to his wife, or his mother-in-law, that he needed to spend more time with his male friends or that he must be about his business even if it meant being away from home for long periods of time. Paul seemed austere and ambitious to a fault. Not many Christians would want him for a husband or father.

My church didn't say sex was bad or evil, only that it was special and should be saved for a special person and a special relationship. I wanted to remain pure, but not forever. I wanted sex to be special, but I needed help for the thoughts that didn't seem special, the desire for someone who wasn't special. The lust for everyone or anyone or all of the opposite sex.

For an adolescent grappling with sex and love, in comparison to the Jewish Bible, the New Testament seemed sexless, almost bloodless. I couldn't look to Mary and Joseph. Mary married Joseph but she didn't make love to him. At least not in the pages of the Bible. This was a role model Christian women seemed to have taken to heart. Or maybe Joseph didn't make love to Mary. Either way, there was a problem for a Christian adolescent in love with love or at least infatuated with his hormones.

I was a Protestant who didn't revere Mary as a virgin, or regard her as one in the long run. The Christian Bible referred to her other children. "Mother of God" seemed blasphemous to me. God was the Mother of God, the Mother and Father of us all. When I was a child, Luke's account of the birth of Jesus seemed right. As an adult writer, I prefer John's ethereal, austere account but not all the time. John is Bach, Luke Beethoven, and when I read either, I think, "Yes, that's the way I would have written it, if I could." To question whether or not Mary was a virgin at the time seems not only trivial but rude and puerile.

Mary was good enough for God and his purpose; she's good enough for me. But as an adolescent, I would have been comforted to know that Joseph sported with Mary, watched her bathe with fascination, or worked fourteen years to get her. I might have been willing to wait fourteen years for my own Rachel.

Both the Bible and tradition presented Mary as a mother, not a wife. I knew of no pictures of Mary kissing Joseph awake, sitting beside him while he worked or putting the kids outside so she and Joseph might have an afternoon to themselves to restore body and soul to their marriage. Tradition pictured Mary as the eternally young, porcelain pale, adoring mother, untouched by work, worry or doubt. It was a portrait I could not identify with.

My favorite story of Mary was when she and her other children tried to rescue Jesus from himself, his mission, because people said he had gone mad. That was a mother I could identify with. "Don't climb too high, son. Don't jump too far. Don't attract attention to yourself."

I would have liked to have such stories about Mary as a wife. Mary and her children telling Joseph, "We want you to come home." Mary telling Joseph, "Put down the hammer and saw and talk to me." Mary looking at Joseph the way she is pictured looking at Jesus.

Joseph seemed to have loved Mary, at least to have had compassion for her, but Mary's love seemed to be reserved for Jesus. Could a woman be both mother and wife? Don't go to the Christian Bible to find out. Paul admonished wives to be submissive to their husbands. Did Paul ever meet Mary? Was Mary submissive to Joseph? All in all, I, and I think most Christian boys, would have preferred Rachel for a wife and maybe for a mother.

I would like to have had one good family role model in the New Testament to show how to handle Potiphar's daughters, Delilah's wanting both your heart and your head, working for one girl and getting another, seeing Bathsheba sunbathing next door.

Like Jeremiah, Jesus didn't marry. If sex wasn't sinful why couldn't there be one story about Jesus loving some girl or even woman? It would have been useful to me for Jesus to have married. To have demonstrated how to deal with the birth of unwanted children, loss of a job, separation, the death of a beloved child, love turned to indifference, work that was more important than family. Most of my heroes left wife and children to discover a new world, or trade route, or business partner, or to conquer the enemy, defend the empire, or take help, healing and Hebrews to the heathen.

I didn't want to read Casanova or Henry Miller. I wanted to read a Bible story about a Christian as pure as Joseph, as playful as Abraham, who finds a wife like Bathsheba, and with her, discovers all the pleasures of Solomon. Instead of instructive stories, I got instructions. All in all, Paul thought celibacy was best but it was better to marry than to burn.

I was burning but I was caught between Scylla and Charybdis. Jesus said anyone who divorced his wife and married another, committed adultery. If I got married, I had better wait until I was smart enough not to make a mistake. On the other hand, Jesus said, anyone who looked at a woman to lust after her committed adultery with her. That made an adulterer of me and every teenage boy who sat in church having Jimmy Carter thoughts about the women in the choir.

Jesus' statement about looking at a woman with lust was a body blow. I was astonished that Jesus knew me that well; I was stricken that I was denied the pleasure and given the pain. Life was not fair. I didn't have my cake or eat it and I still had to do the dishes. I struggled with that guilt for a long time; I couldn't not look. And when I looked, I lusted.

As an adult reader, the Jewish Bible seems to me a book of failures: man's bent to fail, God's intent to redeem. The Christian Bible is a book of failure, redemption, and coming to terms with redemption that looks like failure. The redeemed didn't act much different than the unredeemed. They only pretended to be sexless.

The writers of the Jewish Bible knew more of desperation. There is nothing in the New Testament to equal Job demanding that God justify His ways. Isaiah and Jeremiah knew despair despite their faith that the nation would be resurrected. There isn't that kind of brooding in the New Testament although Jesus does weep over Jerusalem. The Christian Bible has a kind of determined cheerfulness, even in those epistles expecting the imminent end of the world, even in the apocalypse, even in the gospels when the writers knew the crucifixion was coming; they knew the end of the story.

It's like trying to write about the Alamo today. Writers can't convey the shock and horror of the Alamo because they know about San Jacinto. If there had been no San Jacinto, the crucifixion might have some of the despair of Job. Like the Alamo, there is grandeur in the cross rather than gloom.

Jeremiah's most urgent messages were written in poetry. Today, we think of poetry as trivial, esoteric or decorative. The important messages, we believe, are written in deadly serious governmentese, technoise, lawblab or academalarky. We memorize the Thou Shalt Nots and engrave them on our walls.

Jesus' words on divorce came in one of those familiar question and answer episodes that are like verbal wrestling. There is little poetry here and Jesus' statement that remarriage was adultery seems harsh even today. I still have the same wife, but it seems unfair to place such a penalty on someone who might have made an honest, youthful, mistake. It seemed harsh to the disciples who said, "It is good not to marry." And Jesus said, "All men cannot receive this saying, save they to whom it is given." (Matthew 19:11)

Jesus was holding up an ideal and the ideal was equality in marriage. The question had been, "Is it lawful for a man to put away his wife for every cause? And he answered and said unto them, Have ye not read, that he which made them at the beginning made them male and female. And he said, For this cause shall a man leave father and mother, and shall cleave to his wife: and they twain shall be one flesh?" (Matthew 19:3-5)

Jesus takes the high view of creation. Woman was not an afterthought, not a spare rib, not created for the sake of man, but an equal. Man's hardness of heart had made them unequal, but that's not the way God made them. The ideal was the spiritual union of two physical different-but- equal bodies that lasted unto the grave.

Jesus' statement on lusting comes in a compilation of poetry commonly known as the Sermon on the Mount that begins with the beatitudes. "Blessed are the poor in spirit: for theirs is the kingdom of heaven." "Blessed are the meek: for they shall inherit the earth." "Blessed are the peacemakers: for they shall be called the children of God." And it ends, "And it came to pass, when Jesus had ended these sayings, the people were astonished at his doctrine."

That bit of understatement must have caused a few chuckles over the years, following as it did what Christians prefer to believe is eastern exaggeration. "And if any man will sue thee at the law, and take away thy coat, let him have thy cloak also." "But when thou prayest, enter into thy closet." "Take therefore no thought for tomorrow." "And everyone that heareth these sayings of mine, and doeth them not, shall be likened unto a foolish man, which built his house upon the sand."

Christians have spent two thousand years revering Jesus' Sermon on the Mount and rationalizing his meaning. Perhaps Monty Python rationalized best in "The Life of Brian." Blessed are the cheesemakers refers to the makers of all dairy products.

Jesus said, "Ye have heard that it was said by them of old time, Thou shalt not commit adultery: But I say unto you, That whosoever looketh on a woman to lust after her hath committed adultery with her already in his heart. And if thy right eye offend thee, pluck it out, and cast it from thee: for it is profitable for thee that one of thy members should perish, and not that thy whole body should be cast into hell." (Matthew 5: 27-29)

Even allowing for eastern exaggeration, that statement seems a denial of human nature. How else do men look at women? But that's the heart of it. That's the root of women's complaint. That's the politically criminal "lookism." Seeing women as things to be used and possessed. Any man who reduces a woman to a sex object, a thing for his pleasure, is guilty of adultery. Her worth is not restricted or equal to her usefulness to a man. She has worth to herself.

Understanding that resolved one of my adolescent mysteries. I had lusted after my female classmates when they were not around, I had devised stratagems for their seduction when I was alone, but when I was with one of them, I was as courtly as Robert E. Lee. I desired them, but I desired them as women to be loved, not things to be used or possessed. At least, that's my memory.

After one out of town football game, the team and the pep squad girls were allowed to mix on the buses for the return home. When I got off the bus, some of the girls thanked me for being "so nice." That wasn't what I wanted either. Why couldn't I be a dangerous sexual being who was also intelligent and under control?

The Christian Bible replaced laws, that people were scarcely able to keep, with ideals that no one could match. Redemption looked like failure because the redeemed cannot measure up to Jesus' ideal, "By this shall all men know that ye are my disciples, if ye have love one to another" or to Paul's, "There is neither Jew nor Greek, there is neither bond nor free, there is neither male nor female: for ye are all one in Christ Jesus."

Failure can be understood. What cannot be understood is denial. As Southern churches denied freedom to black Christians in the name of God, churches all over the world have denied equality to Christian women in the name of God.

Love is an act. As a noun love is good for nothing but a song. And it doesn't matter whether the song is about women, country or God. Looking at a woman to lust after her is not an act of love. Neither is setting a trap for men. Using a neighbor's service without wages, not proclaiming liberty to your neighbor, not judging the cause of the fatherless. It is not an act of love to God or country to cry "peace" when there is no peace or "justice" when there is no justice. Or to speak pleasing words to gain the favor of rulers or the fame of the crowd.

To look upon a woman and seek to use her person for your pleasure is to commit adultery in your heart. To look upon your country and to lust after its privileges to reserve them to yourself is to commit sedition in your heart. To look upon your religion and to lust after its power to force conformity to your will is to commit blasphemy.

When I read the Bible today I am astonished at how captive our religions have become to our culture. More than captives; they are turncoats. The dominant voice in the land is not the plea for the cause of the fatherless and the right of the needy but the shrill call of the false prophets to worship at the altars of Mammon and Mars. From George Custer to George Patton our heroes are not peacemakers whose lives are characterized by love but are stained with vainglory and blood. From the C.I.A. to the N.R.A. to the K.K.K. our patriots are not poor in spirit but reek of ambition and pride. Our prophets are not reviled for righteousness' sake because they lust after the favor of the crowd.

Our churches pray for the hungry and plea for power and privilege for themselves. From "conquer we must when our cause it is just" to "Oh, the Yankee boys for fighting are the dandy O!" to "He is trampling out the vintage where the grapes of wrath are stored" to "like a mighty army moves the Church of God" to "praise the Lord and pass the ammunition," our anthems praise our self-righteous hate. We have found God and He is us.

City of Fire, Jerusalem ⟶

My excitement at seeing the Israeli flag on the heights over-looking the Jordan River was so obvious that it angered my Jordanian driver. He had been eager to take me to the border but I had wanted to walk across the land bridge between Israel and its enemies. My excitement, even pride at seeing the flag slowly gave way to consternation as I became aware of the heavily fortified border. On the Jordanian side there was no sign of an armed camp, only a ruined refugee village, the walls pitted by gunfire and pocked with holes left by armor piercing shells.

I crossed the border at a very serious looking Israeli bunker. Block upon block of steel-reinforced concrete. It would take several direct hits to knock out the bunker. The Israelis at the border were professional, very careful and very much on guard. There was none of the armed boys attitude I had seen on the Jordanian side. Signs warned of minefields, bunkers guarded the road to Jerusalem.

My first glimpse of the city was a disappointment. Rock hewn Petra was more awe-inspiring. Jerash with its Roman ruins had more grandeur. Amman was less crowded, less frantic.

Sacred to Christians, Muslims and Jews, Jerusalem seemed less a holy place than a guarded city. I saw more guns than churches, synagogues and mosques, more police than priests. Soldiers were on guard outside the place where Jesus was whipped, police outside the church of the Holy Sepulcher. I had to pass a checkpoint to get to the Wailing Wall, another to get to the Mosque of the Dome of the Rock, yet another to reach the Via Dolorosa, the route Jesus is believed to have walked carrying his cross.

Occupation of the west bank permits a degree of security from outsiders the Israelis fear. But there is also fear inside the city.

Many citizens carry guns. Or rocks. The illegal Palestinian flag is painted on walls along with the signs, "Long Live PLO." There were more PLO signs in the Christian Quarter than in the Muslim Quarter of the city. Thirteen percent of Israeli Arabs are Christian. American media had led me to believe Palestinians looked like Arafat. Many looked like those who attended Armenian, Greek Orthodox or Roman Catholic churches in Texas.

Amid the noisy religious protests and political demonstrations were priests reading newspapers in church, students reading the Bible in the Garden tomb, citizens reading books in the outdoor restaurants and bars, tourists examining maps on the crowded streets.

The symbol of Jerusalem is the lion of David but a more accurate symbol might be that of fire. The fire of destruction and rebirth. Jerusalem has repeatedly risen from the ashes.

The fire of inspiration. The revelation of Abraham, of Jesus, of Mohammed inspired many prophets, teachers and poets. Such is the power of the city that poets who have never been there have written about it; artists who have never seen it have painted its scenes. The city also inspired saints and demons, Tartars and Crusaders, pogroms and holocausts, the return of the Jews, the reestablishment of Israel, the creation of the Palestinians.

Jerusalem is a fire that has enlightened the world. It is a fire that smolders, ready to be ignited again, a fire that can combust into light or darkness, that can illuminate or eliminate

Every day, throughout the day, prayers float over the city, carrying with them the guarded hope that the devout and the profane, the political and the religious, pilgrim and tourist, Jew, Muslim and Christian can live together, if not in harmony, at least with order and mutual respect.

Centuries ago a Jew wrote, "Perfect love casts out fear." Does anyone dare believe?

The Combined Platoon ⟶

In December of 1970 and January of 1971, I spent time with Golf Company CUPP (Combined Unit Pacification Program), Second Battalion, Fifth Marines. When I left Vietnam I believed the ARVN with U.S. air support could defend South Vietnam. I believed the peasants the CUPP Marines had trained could defend their homes against the guerrillas. I was not prepared for the political and military collapse of the Republic of Vietnam.

I wondered if I had I misled myself. I also wondered how effective the Combined Unit Pacification Program had been, how it looked to the Vietnamese on either side, and what had happened to the Vietnamese who had been left behind.

In 1989, I returned to Vietnam to find some answers. At that time it was difficult to get there because of the U.S. embargo and difficult to get where you wanted because of the Communist bureaucracy. I went with a group called U.S.-Indochina Reconciliation Project made up of educators. We traveled by land from Phnom Penh to Saigon. For me, and I think for many others, it was a demanding trip, physically and emotionally. I needed time to sort out my feelings and at first things happened too fast. Tan Son Nhut appeared without warning. It was unmarked, with no aircraft overhead to give it away, but you can't hide that much concrete. I thought I saw the old MAC-V compound.

By the time I recognized City Hall, I was at the entrance of the Rex. That was a lot faster than I wanted to go. Officially the hotel was the Ben Thahn, but the stationery, brochure and sign outside identified it as the Rex, just as the city was still called Saigon regardless of the name on the map. Beside the hotel was a small park with a fountain. Once I stood at that fountain and waited for an EOD team to check the building for a bomb.

I went to my room but it was too confining. I went to the rooftop terrace, ordered a beer and, although I hadn't smoked in years, lighted a cigarette. I could see Le Loi and Nguyen Hue, City Hall, the Continental Hotel, the Caravelle, the opera house that became the National Assembly Building for the Republic of South Vietnam and in 1989 showcased rock bands. I spent a very restless night. I was trapped inside myself with thoughts and memories I had buried. Now I was buried with them.

The next morning I decided to see how Ho Chi Minh City differed from Saigon. There were more people, less car traffic in Ho Chi Minh City, with none of the bicycle and motor bikes parked on Le Loi and Nguyen Hue. The squatters shacks along the railroad tracks were gone. In their place a Holiday Inn was being built. Gone also were the blue and white Renault cabs. DeSoto trucks remained, also Lambrettas, pickpockets, cyclos, swarms of children and the homeless. There were fewer ao dais, (traditional female dress, a kind of gown over pajama bottoms) more tee-shirts and jeans. Fewer conical hats, more gimme caps.

We traveled by bus from Saigon past the old bases at Bien Hoa, Long Binh, Phan Rang, Cam Ranh, Nha Trang, Chu Lai. There was a lot more foliage than I remembered along the roads. A man in black pajamas stepped into the road and I jumped, thinking he was V.C. I saw other Vietnamese holding what appeared to be weapons that upon closer inspection were poles, a rolled newspaper, a bicycle pump. A column of smoke rose from the jungle and I had to convince myself it was not a smoke grenade.

Along the road, artillery shells were sometimes used for road markers. Piles of scrap metal lined the road. I examined one of the piles and found crushed steel helmets, mortar rounds, shell casings, gas cans, airplane parts, helicopter doors. An elderly Vietnamese man came over. "American, yes?" he asked. "Americans don't come here anymore," he said sadly. His wife had worked at Chu Lai, what we had called a "hootch maid." He hoped the Americans would come back.

One day we stopped for lunch in Quang Ngai. A crowd of children followed us into the restaurant. The owner tried to run them off but was unsuccessful and the restaurant was so crowded with them we were unable to eat. We went across the road and down a narrow street to an outside table under a tree. The proprietor locked the gate. A crowd gathered to stare over the fence. There was such a crush of curious they broke the chain holding the lock. The proprietor, his wife and mother tried to hold back the crowd but were unable. I ate rice and noodle soup while adults stared and children felt my arms and touched my hair.

Thanh My caught me by surprise. I glimpsed the market and half stood in my seat to look back. Things weren't the same but leaped into consciousness. The bridge, a road, a cemetery, a church, the Song Ba Ren. I had stood on the Ba Ren bridge waiting for helicopters to lift Marines and PF's to an island landing.

This was the place I had come to see, but I wasn't permitted to stop. I saw the mountains and the fence, revetments and pillboxes of Marble Mountain. By the time I got to the hotel in Da Nang I was emotionally exhausted. I could hardly walk upstairs to my room.

The next day as I walked around the city a young man stopped me and pointed at a large Marine emblem on his bicycle. Americans must have given it to him, but why? Had displaying the emblem caused problems? I had no interpreter and he could not understand my questions. A crowd gathered. They had to be reassured several times that I was American and not Russian. They didn't like Russians.

An old man showed me a certificate in English certifying that he was qualified as a heavy equipment operator. "Number one," the others said, holding up a thumb, signifying he was an important person. "Now I am number ten," he said.

They were reluctant to believe that Americans were returning but the idea cheered them. A man brought his tiny daughter. "American," he told her. He wanted her to touch me, but she was afraid.

The city of Hue seemed not to have changed at all, but was perhaps more crowded. I interviewed a doctor at the hospital and rode in a cyclo driven by a former ARVN helicopter pilot. The cyclo driver made as much (money) as the doctor.

Some Vietnamese officials invited me to a drink in the hotel terrace bar. We were discussing politics when suddenly they stopped and turned to look at the television. A musical video was playing and a Vietnamese-American was singing that he wished it were still Saigon while pictures of Saigon flashed on the screen. "We lost you just as you lost your name," he sang. "That is a counterrevolutionary song and this is a government hotel," one of the officials gasped.

From Hue I returned to Da Nang and flew to Hanoi, where I ran into a group of CAP (Combined Action Platoon-the better trained First Marine version of pacification) Marines trying to get back to the villes they had lived in during the war. The group I had come to Vietnam with was going home and I was headed back to Ba Ren and the villes I had been in.

I secured credentials and an interpreter from the Foreign Ministry Press Agency and returned to Da Nang. The interpreter, a woman named Phan Thanh Hao, got a driver and a four-wheel drive vehicle. The interpreter had to introduce me separately to the People's Committee of the Province, District, Commune, and finally, the People's Committee of the hamlet. At each place at least one more official went along to represent me at the next level. Each time I waited in the jeep while the interpreter, a representative of the Foreign Ministry, and members of the Committees explained who I was and what I wanted. Each time it required an hour of protocol before I was brought in and introduced.

After tea was drunk and cigarettes smoked, after a lengthy and flowery introduction, I explained to the People's Committee what the officials had already explained—why I was there and what I wanted. The Committee went into executive session and within a few hours or days, identified the people I would interview. Those persons were told to report to the Committee office.

Because that was intimidating, I received permission to interview the people in their homes. The routine was this: Because I was not permitted to stay overnight in the villes, each morning the interpreter, driver and I left Da Nang and drove into the countryside for the interviews. I was rarely able to do more than three or four interviews a day, sometimes not that many. Always the People's Committee was represented. Often there would be representatives of the People's Committee from the province, district, commune and hamlet. The vehicle was small but three people could ride for a short distance without discomfort. Often six or more passengers sat in each other's laps with others on the hood and roof.

Every interview had a protocol. The host offered tea and the guest offered a gift. Since I traveled with an entourage there were often not enough cups.(The cup was rinsed in lukewarm tea, the tea thrown on the floor and the cup was offered to me.) In one house tea was served on a PX tray, in another on a table made of helicopter parts.

The Foreign Ministry furnished the gifts—cigarettes for adults and candy for the children, to be given by visitors such as myself who were unsophisticated in eastern ways. The Vietnamese were not star-struck and resented having to give time to foreigners so the press center paid them to insure their cooperation. I'm glad I did not know that at the time.

Members of the Peoples Committee were present to introduce me, assure the subjects they could talk to me and to tell them what I wanted. They also acted as guides, an important function because after 1975, many of the names of the hamlets and villages were changed and the districts and provinces realigned. Sometimes it was necessary to resort to old U.S. military maps which I had brought in order to determine which hamlet I wanted to visit.

When a village was in another district, it was necessary to go to the People's Committee of that district. Although only a few kilometers away it might be a couple of hours by road and after arriving it was necessary to make an appointment for the following day.

Because there were no restaurants in the hamlets, the Committee designated a family to provide the noon meal for me, the interpreter, driver, officials and family of the host. During one meal, the interpreter left the house, leaving me in effect voiceless.

Later she told me the food was so bad she could not eat it. She didn't tell me I had the same choice.

I was a curiosity in the hamlets, perhaps more so because of my entourage, and people followed me everywhere. When I had to relieve myself, I informed the officials who formed a human shield providing some privacy.

The crowd followed me into the house of the person I was interviewing. Those who could not crowd into the house packed the doorway and windows when there were windows, making it so dark inside it was difficult to take notes and so noisy that it was difficult to tape record the interviews. During one interview it was necessary, because of the crowd, to move to another house. The crowd moved with me. In another, officials used bamboo sticks to drive women and children out of the house, creating bedlam. I did not see them use sticks on any men and the women and children returned as quickly as they left.

It was also difficult, in front of family, friends, neighbors and officials to ask questions that could cause embarrassment or trouble to the subject. I interviewed a woman who said she had been raped by Americans. I was interviewing her in front of her family, relatives, neighbors. I interviewed a police interrogator. Crowded around in the hootch were people he had interrogated and sometimes tortured and relatives of some he had interrogated who had not returned to the ville.

In some instances, neighbors or officials answered a question before the subject could. Perhaps the answers were correct, but no subject argued with the answer given by an official. Sometimes the crowd reacted to questions with laughs, grunts or other sounds that also may have affected the answer. It was politically impossible to conduct private interviews so all the interviews have to be viewed with some suspicion.

The Vietnamese were unable to identify what American unit had been present at what time. They also overestimated the size of American forces and American bases. They observed a lunar calendar so dates had to be calculated, adding more uncertainty to the inaccuracy of memory.

The subjects were not scientifically selected, nor were there enough of them to form a definitive picture. The subjects were from the hamlets I had been in during the war, both those in the friendly villes I lived in and those in the guerilla area I visited while accompanying CUPP teams on their operations. The subjects were selected by the various Peoples Committees who had their own agenda. There were people they wanted me to see, stories they wanted me to hear, and perhaps they did not entirely understand what I wanted. They were eager to help, but I kept in mind that they decided who I talked to and they were always present.

Nguyen Trung opposed the French from 1945 to 1954 and was secretary of the Youth Union in his village. After the Geneva agreement in 1954, he was a village teacher. In 1965 the village was "liberated" by guerrillas (Viet Cong). Trung became head master at the primary school of the revolutionaries from 1965 to 1968. Then the Americans built a base nearby and the war was so terrible that Trung left the school and moved to the area of the republicans (the area controlled by Saigon). The republicans knew he had been a revolutionary and forced him to be a recruiter in what we would have called Psychological Operations.

His staff was equipped with a loud speaker and leaflets. In the secure area they walked and threw leaflets or rode in a jeep and used the loudspeaker. In insecure areas, helicopters dropped leaflets. Some guerrillas joined the Saigon forces.

As a recruiter he was successful because after Tet in 1968, even the remotest hamlets were bombed. Some guerrillas couldn't bear it any more. He asked them to join the ARVN and many joined the Chieu Hoi program. Some former guerrillas, if of high rank, worked with the Americans. The numbers joining depended on living conditions. There were two groups: those who wanted to follow Saigon and those who had to be checked to see if they joined the guerrillas again.

Trung was in reeducation camp for nine years because he had defected and then recruited other defectors. He was suspected of being CIA. Some were still in the camp when he left after nine years because of their high position in the military or government or because they illegally left the country. At least one was returned to detention after being released.

I was told several times by the Peoples Committees and by both those who were guerrillas and those who were ARVN that no Americans had lived in the villes. I was told about one American who was hidden by the guerrillas for a time and then taken to North Vietnam. No one could remember his name but it appeared to be Robert Garwood who was captured in 1965, returned to the United States in 1979, and was found guilty of desertion and collaborating with the enemy in 1981.

One day, the driver stopped under a tree where a young man sold drinks and cigarettes. The members of the Peoples Committee were thirsty. The young man operating the shop recognized me as an American and spoke to me in English. His name was Dang Nam and he remembered the Marines who lived in the hamlet.

He first met them when he was eight-years-old. His family was eating and they asked his mother the name of the food. They taught each other to speak. He said, "We don't talk to each other so well, but I know very well the name of the crackers."

The Marines called him "Mickey" and he and the other children followed them. The Marines played cards, went swimming and kicked a ball with the children and tried to teach them chess. They gave them food and crackers and at Christmas time, "that means on the 24th of December," he said, they gave the children toys. "They lived in this village, but they lived from house to house; they moved every day. In the morning they stay in this house and in the evening they moved to another house. At night they go to their patrol."

I think the Peoples Committee did not believe Americans could live in the villes. They may have also misunderstood the question, or perhaps the translation. Americans stayed in the villes but didn't live there. Maybe that's what they meant. One former guerilla told me, "The Americans lived in the hamlets but we lived among the people."

Dang Nam told me the Marines prevented the young people from following the revolutionaries. When the Americans were in his house, they treated him normally. The family let the Marines have the main room and moved into the smaller one. Half of the room was filled with canned food. He said the Marines worried about resupply during the rainy season and stored food.

The children's parents tried to prevent them from following the Americans because they were afraid the children would be caught in the nearby fighting. He said he had heard of the "sliding platoon" but it was not the same as the ones who stayed in the ville. The older boys joined the revolutionaries at the very last but he was too young. He did not know what had happened to the PFs who fought with the Marines.

Tan Trinh, Chairman of Que My Commune, grew up during the "Diem revenge" against the revolutionaries. "A lot of people were killed then but the hardest time was 1970 to 1972 when 1,267 guerrillas were killed by a "sliding platoon." He believed the men in the platoon carried others on their back with netting over them so that there appeared to be fourteen but in reality there were twenty-eight. When they left, they carried bags of the same size filled with air, so that they all seemed to leave but actually half the men stayed behind to ambush the guerrillas.

I heard this story from several sources but it's hard for me to imagine an American in full combat gear carrying another American in full combat gear across paddies or over the dikes or trails.

Trinh said he fought against the Americans in this area, and the cruelest and most barbarous unit was the sliding platoon. Their main military bases were the Bat Cave and Que Mountain.

The Bat Cave was LZ Baldy, headquarters of the Second Battalion. I assumed that Que Mountain, also called The Rock, was of equal size, headquarters of First Battalion, Hill 34. The guerrillas spoke of The Rock with a respect bordering on reverence, saying they attacked it many times but were never able to take it. In fact, the Rock was a CUPP platoon Command Post where I had spent some time.

Trinh remembered the Vietnamese combined with Americans in fighting units but none of the Vietnamese remained. Either they were killed in the war or they moved away because they were so useful to the Americans in fighting the guerrillas. They were not killed after liberation but perhaps they moved away after reeducation.

In one hootch while I was interviewing, someone said behind me in perfect English, "Hello, how are you?" Because so many people were pressed against me, I was unable to turn and spot the English speaker.

Outside, while I was walking down a footpath, surrounded by the people who crowded the house, the man again said, "Hello, how are you?" I asked where he learned English. "I was a teacher for the Americans," he said. "Now I am a leper," he said. "A leper," he repeated. I said I wanted to talk to him. He walked away through the crowd. I called after him. He didn't stop. The Committee could force him to talk to me but that might cause him difficulties with the officials or with his neighbors.

I decided to risk it. The Committee said they did not know who he was and anyway he was gone and was perhaps crazy. We were on a path in a hamlet accessible only by foot. It was impossible that he was a stranger or that the officials did not know who he was. The Committee knew where everyone was at every moment. Who was he? What was his story? I will never know.

A few days later I was interviewing in a crowded hootch. The interpreter was sick. I couldn't breathe and Vietnamese crowded in until I was bent double over the small table. Le Van Luong said he had seen me several times at "The Rock" and asked if I was in the military. I believed he was lying, trying to ingratiate himself because I was never at Hill 34 that (I) thought was "The Rock."

He had been recruited as an ordinary soldier and was accidentally shot by a comrade when both were drunk. He was sent home where he was helped by local authorities to return to farming. He assisted the Marines as honcho, cut their hair, accompanied them on operations and communicated with them in half

English, half Vietnamese. Liberation by North Vietnam came peacefully to the hamlet and he was not sent to reeducation camp.

I asked about the boys who served as translators and the "Bicycle Bettys," the girls who rode bicycles between the villes, sold Cokes to the Marines and sometimes informed them of the movement of the Viet Cong. Luong said the boys were killed in the war or moved away, the girls married Americans or moved away. I believed he was unreliable and therefore did not ask many questions I could have asked.

The next to the last day in the area, I was taken to Happy Valley. On the way I saw on a hilltop a large boulder bearing a Marine emblem and recognized it as the Platoon CP. I asked the driver to stop and the Peoples Committee explained that was Que Mountain or The Rock that had been attacked many times but never taken. I asked to interview Luong again but was told it was impossible. The Committee would have to meet, he would have to be notified, the protocol would take too long. That was my biggest failure of the entire trip.

Disturbed by what I had heard about the "sliding platoons," I met with Le Cong Co, Deputy Head of the National Fatherland Front, a member of the National Assembly and principal of the Foreign Language Center in Da Nang. Born in Da Nang, he joined the revolutionary forces when he was fourteen and for twenty-one years, from 1954 to 1975, was involved in revolutionary activities.

The National Liberation Front was founded in 1960 and Le Cong Co organized a federation of students in central Vietnam and was its head. There were two kinds of organizations, an official one called the General Association of Students and the revolutionary organization. He organized the revolutionary students into a federation that mobilized the political struggle and demonstrated against the Americans in 1964 and 1966.

I asked Co about the sliding platoon. He said he was almost killed several times by the sliding platoon. The "crawling platoon" was different from the sliding platoon. I think by crawling platoon he meant infantry. "The 'diving Americans' dived into the water to ambush us," he said. "Those diving under the water belonged to the Marine infantry forces." Force Recon did have scuba-trained teams or they could have been SEALs. He said the sliding platoons belonged to the Marine infantry force and were organized in Phu Bai. The pacification program was called The Phu Bai Experiment.

"They were good soldiers," he said. "One afternoon, I observed a sliding platoon from a hill with my binoculars. Three were put there as guardians. For two hours they stood still. They were guerrillas like us. When they were sliding they fulfilled their duty very well. We were killed a lot because of them because they had good order and good discipline."

He said, "The area that you have visited we called the 'mixing area,' occupied by the republicans during daytime and by the revolutionary force during nighttime. This sliding platoon gathered the people into concentrated areas beside the stations. These Americans immersed themselves in people's gardens. If the guerrillas came back to get rice or information this platoon killed them. Then they knew the house that the guerrillas entered and they killed all the people inside that house. This platoon was organized to fulfill these kinds of duties. These Americans were in charge of eliminating the people who supplied the V.C. Even in a certain area called 'free fire zone' people could live underground. But when the sliding platoon appeared the ordinary people had to leave that area. The sliding platoons were successful."

The Marines did set ambushes for guerrillas coming into the villes. They also ambushed houses where guerrillas met but I knew of no incidents where they entered the houses of spies, couriers or saboteurs and killed them. I did witness the capture or arrest of one high-ranking guerrillas by CUPP Marines. He was turned over to the Vietnamese PFs who greeted him like a relative and took him to Hoi An for interrogation. Nevertheless, the story of Marines entering houses and killing the occupants troubled me.

By accident in Da Nang I ran into two of the CAP Marines I had met in Hanoi. They and the photographer accompanying them told of their reunions with the people of the hamlets in which they lived. That did not sound like the fearsome sliding platoon.

My time in Vietnam was running out but I asked to be taken to a hamlet where the Marines had returned. I was taken by sampan to a small fishing village and the house of a man whose mother was killed by Koreans. The hamlet was revolutionary and no Americans lived there nor had any come there since the war. I said again that I wanted to talk to the people the Americans visited.

I was taken to meet Dang Thung, a barber. His father was one of the leaders of the "free" village. Either he hadn't learned the party vocabulary or he was defying the party line that this was an "occupied" rather than "free" village. The Marines first came in 1968, lived in the village and mixed with the people. Thung worked with them in a council. He pointed out another man who was village chief and worked with the Marines as "honcho."

Thung remembered "See rate" who was sergeant and Bill who had just returned to see him. Bill was a joyful man. After his patrol he used to play with the children. "Nam", apparently a nickname, was a corpsman. When children or fishermen caught a cold or couldn't breathe, Nam called helicopters to take them to the hospital to be cured. A lot of people were injured in the fighting. Those who were seriously injured were sent to Hoi An. Those who were still alive came back. Those who died were buried and the family informed so that they could come and retrieve the body.

When the Marines returned, they asked to see him. He said, "I was glad to see them because we were old friends a long time ago and now we met each other again. It was joyful."

He said, "The People's Committee were surprised that the Marines came back. They came here with a woman photographer as a memory of our meeting after seventeen years. They asked about the children who had helped them. Only one was alive. The Americans brought candy for the children and for the old women Salem cigarettes."

I told Trung that I could not find any of the children who assisted the Marines or any of the bicycle girls. Trung thought they moved. "As for me, I think that. I just tell you the truth. There is nothing to be hidden."

The Peoples Committee was chagrined that the Americans were welcomed with such enthusiasm and joy, but I was relieved.

One footnote: While I was in Cambodia I had an interview with General Te Bahn, Minister of Defense. In 1989, the Vietnamese were leaving Cambodia and the Khmer Rouge was threatening to return. I asked Bahn how his army was going to defend remote villages against the Khmer Rouge.

He said the Vietnamese Army had been training platoons of Cambodian soldiers who would live in the villages and train the people to defend the village. The Vietnamese believed the Combined Action Platoon was such a success they were imitating the program in Cambodia.

Understanding Vietnam ⟶

War has always been hard to understand. Why here? Why now? Why in this way? And, above all, why in the name of God and humanity can't we seem to live without it?

War has also been hard to explain. Writing about war to someone who has never been in war is like explaining marriage to a eunuch. It's a different world. It's a doubly different world because military life is already difficult enough to explain, and wartime military life is distinctly different from peacetime military life.

It's particularly difficult to explain war to Americans because most Americans know little of war. Except for those at Pearl Harbor, no living native-born American has seen bombs falling on his neighborhood, enemy troops marching down his street, or tanks rolling across his lawn. Most American citizens do not know what war looks like or feels like or smells like. It is doubly difficult to explain war to Americans because, unfortunately, we think we do know.

We think we know what war is like because we live in the age of information and we have the facts. We have seen war as it has been represented by artists. We have seen paintings of the sweep and grandeur of battle, with flags waving and generals prancing on white horses. But the lines are too clean, the colors too bright, and no matter how accurate, paintings convey none of the stench, the incredible carnage, the shrieks and moans of the frightened, the wounded, and the dying.

We have read poems glorifying heroes and heard the songs of the victors. Poetry, trapped in its very form, lends refinement to horror, as in Dylan Thomas's "A Refusal to Mourn the Death, by fire, of a Child in London," or a pattern of pleasure to meaningless pain, as in Randall Jarrell's "Death of the Ball Turret Gunner." Rhythmical, rational, systematic, poetry cannot capture the sprawling chaos of war.

Fiction writers, at least those who are after understanding rather than spoils, are caught in drama, narrative drive, and the other elements of a good story, the form more important than the function. They must challenge the appealing heroics of Homer and Shakespeare and describe the grotesque and obscene without driving away the sickened reader. Unlike poetry, fiction must appeal to masses who have not been trained to recognize truth, much less applaud it.

Some citizens, perhaps, have heard the scabrous stories of warriors whose tongues are unfamiliar with heroics, and virtue, and the righteousness of their cause, but such stories seem pointless, and the warriors retire into obscurity, their medals tarnished with the memory of what they have seen and done.

Generals write books filled with grandiose schemes, fantastic strategies, and glorious and meaningful triumphs.

Journalism offers limited ways of seeing selected pictures, and most easily follows the path of counting the dead, weighing the bombs, and measuring progress and loss in dollars and feet.

History, eventually, attempts to put the puzzle together in a rational scheme, for those who read history, and to answer the who and how and where and when, but never the why.

The movies combined the sweep and grandeur of painting with the heroics and songs of the poets and became the propaganda arm of the government to give us good and evil based on the color of one's uniform. Everyone in German or Japanese uniform was bad, and the death of each one of them made the world a better place in which to live. Italians were bad too, but you could feel sorry for them if you also felt contempt.

However, the movies did not explain that many war criminals wore no uniform at all. Or that many of those on both sides who did wear uniforms were unwilling warriors, caught up by force of law, or patriotism, or some personal need for escape from present misery or private misgiving. The movies did not explain evil men who looked like ourselves. But the movies gave us real made-in-Hollywood carnage, real safe-in-Hollywood courage, real money-in-the bank patriotism.

It was not just that the actors pretended hunger, or fear, or courage, but they pretended to know, pretended to have experienced, and, therefore, pretended authority for telling others what war was like. Houses were burned in war, whole cities of them; children were killed, whole schools of them. But not by Americans. Only the implacably evil Germans and Japanese killed civilians on the screen.

Poets and painters gave us war as a terrible beauty. Fiction writers gave us war as a palatable tale of drama and import. Journalism gave us war as facts, lists, places, men and materiel. Warriors gave us war as pointless anecdote. Generals gave us war as the moral equivalent of free enterprise. History gave us war as compressed biography.

The movies gave us innocence. The painters, poets, journalists, generals, and historians had said otherwise. They had pointed at an America that knew wars for economic advantage and political gain, that knew slavery, and after slavery, sweat shops, child labor, and the importation of immigrants to maintain the semblance of slavery; an America that knew Antietam, Sand Creek, Dresden, and Hiroshima. But the movies gave us real made-in-Hollywood innocence. And we basked in that innocence. And we believed we knew.

Then came Vietnam. War in our living rooms. Television gave us death in living color, with the screen a stage for the most outrageous and attention-getting sound bite. We saw professional soldiers playing the beast and the clown to grab ten seconds of the nation's attention that was focused on the screen. We saw men in American uniforms who looked the way the enemy was supposed to have looked, men who didn't die on glorious fields of battle but in mud, in filth, in unhallowed ground their comfortable patriots would not walk on. Men who were not John-Wayne tough, or Ronald-Reagan righteous. Men who did not glory in the job their country had given them of killing other men, or delight when the job was well done.

It wasn't My Lai that showed us the face behind our innocent masks; it was Washington, and Wall Street, and that eye in the living room. War wasn't like this in the movies. War had never been presented like this by those who heroically and patriotically stayed behind to help civilian morale and to pick up loose change. And the shock went deep. What had happened to our children? What had happened to America?

War is difficult to understand. That's why we link killing for political and economic causes with quasi-religious slogans, like killing some men to free others, or waging war to end war. In the best wars, the good wars, the holy wars, the linkage holds, at least for true believers.

The war in Vietnam is the latest war we can't understand. We thought we knew; we had seen it in the movies. We can't understand, because John Kennedy's linkage—to bear any burden, meet any hardship, support any friend, oppose any enemy in the name of liberty—was applauded as poetry but not as practice. And because no one ever defined what was at stake, or what our interest was, or what would constitute victory.

We can't, and don't, understand because we can't accept that war was always like this. We would have to give up our dream of good wars, of righteous killing, have to give up Ivanhoe, Natty Bumppo, Scarlett O'Hara's brave idealistic and tragic Ashley, and John Wayne and his affably innocent sidekick, Ronald Reagan. We'd have to give up heroic warriors who never suffered doubt or diarrhea, who killed without remorse and triumphed without guilt. And with only a backward glance at their fallen comrades and enemies. "Sorry about that, pilgrim."

Vietnam was not an aberration. Vietnam was irregular, exceptional and strange.

Vietnam was irregular because many enemy soldiers were irregulars, guerrillas, without uniforms or insignia, indistinguishable from civilians. And many "non-combatants" acted as spies, couriers, recruiters and suppliers of the enemy. They planted mines and boobytraps. My Lai was a terrible atrocity and one from which we tried to recoil, as though it were not a part of us. We had become accustomed to distant massacres of civilians by bombs, even fire and atomic bombs. We had been in denial of close range atrocities by rope, musket and rifle. "The only good one is a dead one," "Nits make lice," and "lynch law" are as American as "Praise the Lord and pass the ammunition."

In the American Civil War, irregulars were executed. Thomas Martin, sixteen, was shot as a guerrilla by a Union firing squad because when he enlisted near the end of the war the Confederates had no uniforms. Martin had to furnish his own rifle. In Vietnam, terrorists and guerrillas received the same treatment as the uniformed soldiers of North Vietnam.

Vietnam was exceptional in that the rules of engagement were exceptionally stringent. Perhaps in part because of the television cameras. Could General Sherman have marched to the sea if television cameras had been present? Would Sherman and Sheridan have been war criminals in the nightly news?

Spies and those who aided and sheltered spies were ignored or treated as political prisoners. In peace time America, the Rosenbergs were executed for spying. Two assistants received thirty and fifteen years in prison. Lord Haw Haw was executed, Axis Sally spent twenty years in jail, and Tokyo Rose spent seven for war-time propaganda.

As a young Marine in the Korea era, I was trained to never let prisoners outnumber me. If there were three of us and four of the enemy surrendered, we were to shoot three and take one prisoner. In Vietnam that would have been murder. In Vietnam a uniformed American teenager could be shot on sight; un-uniformed Vietnamese teenagers carrying messages or military supplies could not. In Vietnam I observed Marines unable to call an artillery or air strike on a suspected ambush site because maps showed a village in the area. The village had been relocated and nothing remained as evidence there had been a village; hootches had dirt floors and no foundations. Nevertheless, if ambushed it was impossible for the Marines to direct fire on the area.

In Vietnam there was no firebombing of cities as in Tokyo or Dresden. One of the icons of Vietnam is the photograph of a screaming girl, burned naked by napalm, fleeing a burning village. It might have been instructive if the text had mentioned that the village was under attack by the Viet Cong, that the village chief ordered the village evacuated and requested South Vietnamese airplanes to bomb the Viet Cong. Unknown to anyone, ten frightened children had hidden in the village rather than fleeing it. There was no American involvement but the photograph hangs exceptionally heavy in the American conscience.

Vietnam was strange because the major American victory, the battles of Tet 1968 that virtually destroyed the Viet Cong, was a propaganda and therefore a political defeat.

Vietnam was strange to the American experience. Americans had fought guerrillas in the Philippines and Nicaragua but never before had they fought an enemy that attempted to draw their fire upon civilians before fleeing to the countryside. Never before had the enemy had safe havens not only across borders but inside the country. Unlike Europe where churches were shelled and Monte Cassino bombed, Vietnam had sacred places where the enemy could recuperate and Americans could not pursue.

Americans had fought in jungles before but World War Two soldiers were largely rural; mules, cows, pigs, flies were ordinary. Recruits were intimate with poverty, hunger and despair. Army chow looked good after depression bread lines. Sleeping in a foxhole wasn't vastly different from sleeping in a boxcar or under a bridge.

Vietnam soldiers were city boys who were accustomed to cars, television, soap and easy money; more familiar with playing in the streets than playing in the woods. A pig in the yard was unusual; a water buffalo was surreal. Flies and mosquitoes were not customary; filth, poverty and disease were not normal; snakes, leeches, monsoons, living and sleeping in mud were not natural. They were more at home in a helicopter than in a rice paddy, more comfortable in a PX than in a village that had no streets, no traffic, no TVs, no toilets; where houses were not lined up but scattered under trees and folds of the earth.

Many World War Two soldiers had slaughtered pigs or chickens for food, perhaps participated in the burial of parents or siblings. Death was oblique to many of the soldiers sent to Vietnam. Few of them were acquainted with violent death. Those who had smelled blood had witnessed an athletic contest or perhaps a schoolyard fight.

Vietnam was not an anomaly. Vietnam, like Korea, was a hot battle of the Cold War that began when Stalin failed to keep the Yalta agreement regarding postwar settlement of the occupied territories. In 1947, Truman proclaimed the Truman Doctrine and supported Turkey, Greece and Iran against Communist insurgents. In 1948, Truman authorized the Berlin Airlift when the Soviets cut off access to the city. In 1950, Truman ordered U.S. troops to fight under the flag of the United Nations in Korea and sent military advisors to Vietnam. Congress approved the North Atlantic Treaty Organization or NATO agreement.

In 1952, when Eisenhower announced $60 million dollars in aid to French forces in Vietnam the United States was paying three-fourths of the cost of the war. In 1954, congress approved the Southeast Asia Treaty Organization, or SEATO agreement pledging to defend South Vietnam. Presidents Truman, Eisenhower, Kennedy, Johnson, Nixon, Ford, Carter and Reagan enlisted America in the Cold War and every congress after 1947 supported it.

No doubt historians will long argue whether the Cold War was necessary or wise, whether Korea and Vietnam were worth the cost, but they were not futile. There can be no doubt who won the war. It may be that the Cold War did more to determine the contour of the world in the Twenty-First Century that either World War One or Two.

No doubt historians will long argue the causes for the collapse of the Soviet Union but there can be little doubt that the first cracks in the Iron Curtain were made by the Truman Doctrine, the Berlin Airlift and the hot wars in Korea and Vietnam. Politicians will take their bows, but it is long past time to pay respect to the forgotten soldiers of Korea and the dishonored soldiers of Vietnam whose country asked them to defend others from tyranny.

It is long past time to abandon the pretense that there are "clean" wars or "good" wars, or "holy" wars. There are no good wars. War may be necessary but it is a calamity to all who are involved. We don't kill ideas, or demons, or mad men. We kill flesh and blood soldiers who die for comrades and country, and non-combatants caught in the crossfire of famine, disease, fear, rage and revenge.

We can thank God that Vietnam was not a popular war, not a crusade of good against evil. We can pray America never again fights a "good" war. Nothing is more destructive than a popular war where children cheer, and the pious pray, for the death of the enemy. When evil dies, what becomes of us?

Hooked on Heroes ⸺

The first truth in war is casualties. You never get over the losses.

Desert Storm was my fourth war, not counting such diversions as Nicaragua, Lebanon, Libya, Grenada and Panama. It was my fifth war if I count the losses, because my father was in World War One, and his losses were my losses too.

Although he escaped maiming, my father's life was shortened by pneumonia and mustard gas, and he had nightmares the rest of his life. He kept a newspaper clipping of one of those nightmares. "Twenty-six men of this unit (Company A, 360th Infantry) survived the half hour's fighting November 2. Two hundred and ten men entered the fight." He also kept his moth-eaten doughboy uniform with its campaign ribbons and battle stars. As a child tempted by invincibility, I studied that clipping and uniform and hoped that somewhere in me was the fortitude to go over the top and continue to advance in the face of catastrophe, to achieve with courage and will what could not be done by flesh and blood.

I was a child during World War Two and I waved at troop trains, marked progress on a map by pasting American flags on towns and islands. I collected scrap metal, bought war stamps until I had enough to exchange for a war bond, attended services for those who would never return, and watched wives and mothers place gold stars in their windows.

Hooked on heroes, madmen, and good wars, I learned many of my values then. Allied soldiers were good. Japanese and Germans were inhuman and deserved an agonizing death. I cheered newsreels of bombs falling on Germany and of the flaming bodies of Japanese soldiers. I learned to hate as a patriotic and religious duty. I learned to love destruction, the power and release of it. I learned that wrong, and wrong-thinking people, had to be set right, most often by violence. Might meant right, and even when it didn't, it meant money.

My father was troubled by the pleasure, self-righteousness and profit that I, and others, were getting from the war. He believed we should never fight another war, that wars never ended wars. Although he despised the German government, he felt sympathy for his old enemy, the German soldier who tried to continue in the face of catastrophe. He would not go to movies where audiences cheered Ronald Reagan and other celluloid heroes who sneered at the enemy and mowed them down like melons. I was embarrassed by my father's lack of patriotism. I feared the war would end before I was old enough to dispatch a Nip.

I was old enough for Korea and I promptly enlisted in the Marines. I didn't go to Korea and I considered that a loss, almost a moral loss. But, if by education we mean forming a coherent and comprehensive world view, the Marine Corps was the best school I ever attended. If by education we mean understanding: the forces that shaped western civilization, the ways in which we form moral and ethical values, the process of human thinking, the ways in which science and technology are applied to human needs, the interactions between human behavior and social processes, the Marine Corps was the best school I attended. If by education we mean learning who we are, what is real and what it means to be a human being, the Marine Corps is second to none.

The Marines taught me a respect for military hardware and a delight in using it. They taught me ways to kill, and that I could do so easily and without many qualms. Killing comes easily to humans, so easily that some brood about it forever after.

Unable to go to Vietnam as a Marine, I went briefly as a reporter and returned home with my own nightmares and contradictions. The government of North Vietnam was as repressive as totalitarian governments any place. The people of South Vietnam deserved liberty as much as people anywhere. The soldiers of both sides were as brave as soldiers have ever been and their courage and will proved nothing.

I also returned to find a nation addicted to the vicarious enjoyment of violence. When television news was unable to provide exploding vehicles, burning houses and torn and bleeding bodies, movies and television shows rushed in to fill the need. But it was never entirely satisfactory. Politicians, unable or unwilling to give bread and education to the masses, gave us the expensive but edifying circus: Nicaragua, Lebanon, Libya, Grenada, Panama, the Persian Gulf. They were thrilling teasers for the main event.

When the shooting started in Iraq, I was Velcroed to the tube. So were many other men and women. And children. That's one of the losses. A friend asked if I thought it was a mistake. I did. He asked if I wished I were there. I did. I consider that one of the losses.

You never forget a war. You never get over the losses. And no one ever wins. Sometimes it's necessary not to lose a war. Sometimes there's nothing to be won. Whatever it is you think you win, it's not superiority. That's one of the losses.

Sullen

India, the Divided Crowd ⟿

It is no wonder that India is the land of meditation and contemplation. India overwhelms your senses. The sights, sounds, smells, tastes are more than you can absorb. The noise assaults you. Traffic, people shouting, temple bells, Muslim calls to prayer, hawkers and vendors yelling in your ear.

No one could wish a larger population for India. It is hard to forgive Mother Teresa for saying Indian women should have as many children as God will give them. She eased the suffering of hundreds and increased the suffering of millions. The government recognizes the problems of overpopulation but both the government and the citizens lack the resources for birth control.

Both Muslims and Hindus are in a population race for majority control. And, as in China, there is a problem of infanticide. Female babies are sometimes killed. If parents can have only one or two children, they want them to be males. Females are seen as a burden. Marriages are arranged, usually before the girl reaches puberty, and a girl's parents must pay a dowry. A family with only female children can be impoverished by marriages. A family with only male children profits when those sons marry. Although the government has made a determined effort to stop the practice, in the country brides are sometimes killed by their in-laws so that the son may marry again and bring another dowry to the family.

The plight of women is not a happy one. In villages men stand and talk or sit and drink tea while women lift heavy loads. The women tend the fields, do the cooking, care for the house and the children. They also fetch the water, which means walking to the village well and carrying a container of water on their head. Water weighs eight pounds per gallon, forty pounds for five gallons. Indian women are small but some of them carry a container of water in each hand with another container on their head. When we were entertained by village dancers the women danced with bowls on their heads, stacked seven high. It was good training for girls who would someday have to carry water for their husbands.

Women are not encouraged to get an education. Although the constitution declares that all citizens are equal, it doesn't work out that way. The government requires that women be represented in the government, but often the husband of a woman who has been elected to an office acts as her proxy, going to meetings and voting in her stead.

In 1853, the British outlawed suttee or sati, the practice of burning a widow on her husband's funeral pyre, but it still exists. Sati means good woman. Houses of women who have committed sati have a mark where the woman dipped her hand in henna or another dye and left her hand print on the house before burning to death. A good woman. Ajay, our guide, said widows had no place to go—meaning no where but beggary and prostitution. After one Mogul victory in battle 30,000 women are supposed to have committed sati. There is a monument to a woman who committed sati with her three children. A good woman.

There is a struggling woman's movement. In a village, a bride was raped by her father-in-law. The bride attempted to kill herself and failing to do so confessed to her grandmother-in-law. The grandmother went to the police who did nothing. The bride's father insisted the bride kill herself and swore that if she didn't he would kill her to restore the family's honor so that her brothers and sisters could marry. The village women demanded justice, and despite threats, punished the father and the father-in-law and restored the dignity of the bride.

It is not the government that denies equality, but religion. Neither Muslims nor Hindus regard women as being equal. In addition, Hindus have a rigid caste system. You are born into a caste and it determines your occupation, your status, when and whom you can marry, your diet, and, in some places, where you can walk. When the British built roads and railroads in India there was great concern that all castes could walk on the same road or ride together on the same train.

No matter how intelligent you are, how courageous, creative, devout, there is nothing you can do that could change your caste. Except convert to Islam or Christianity. Sikhs, a reformed off-shoot of Hinduism, also do not recognize the caste system. For others, the castes are self-governing. They punish anyone who attempts to rise above his station by marrying or accepting a job outside his caste. Any children resulting from a mixed caste marriage belong to the caste of the lower caste spouse. Hindus believe that their caste is due to a previous life and it is essential to accept and live according to one's station in order to attain a higher caste in the next life.

In the Treaty of Paris, 1763, ending The French and Indian War in America and the Seven Year War in Europe, the French gave up all claim to Canada and India. The British established a monopoly in trade for the East India Company. The East India Company ran the country using Indian soldiers led by British officers. Hindu soldiers would not take orders from Muslims or from Indians of a lower caste but higher military rank.

• • •

The streets of cities and villages of India were lined with men with nothing to do. At night or early in the morning they huddled over small, smoky fires of discarded wood and paper. Although starvation had been eliminated, people, especially men, slept on the street, slept on the ground, even in day time, even in the business areas of the city. One family had set up a tent in a trash pile in New Delhi. The children combed the trash for usable or edible items.

Indians walked in the street because most often there was no sidewalk and where there was a sidewalk, vendors and hawkers had taken up the space. And there were beggars. Mostly children. "Hello, hello," they shouted.

We could not refrain from speaking to them and when we did, "Hello, pen," they shouted. "Hello, pen." Ajay said that they had pens but previous tourists had given them pens so they asked for them. He requested that we not give the children anything. As we walked along streets we collected children, all of them shouting, "Hello, pen." Occasionally Ajay said to them in Indian, "Enough," and a few left.

Hardest to ignore were tiny young women with babies who gestured at the baby's mouth asking food for their children. Were they single parents? Wives of worthless men? Widows trying to avoid sati for themselves and their children? Ajay didn't know but asked us not to encourage begging. Yet, every day we left soap and shampoo in the hotel to be discarded and passed people begging for those items. Gypsies along the road rubbed their heads as we passed, asking for shampoo. Too late I realized we should have collected the hotel soap, shampoo, lotion and given it to Ajay to distribute. He lived there; he must know how to do charity.

The vendors also shouted, "Hello, hello." When I responded it was a signal to intrude in my space, impede my progress, and shout in my ear while placing items in my hand. If I looked at the item or took it for fear that it would fall and break I was lost. They wouldn't take it back but shouted prices. If I offered half or a third of the price, I was surrounded by other hawkers who had the same item for less. I had to fight my way through them. Occasionally Ajay again said to them in Indian, "Enough," and a few left.

Ajay explained that although it seemed discourteous, it was best not to speak to the vendors and not to look at their wares unless we wanted to buy. It worked but then we didn't get a chance to look at things we might want to buy, and if we made a close inspection it was difficult to escape the vendors without pushing them aside. They seemed to accept this without offense but it seemed aggressive and ugly American as I was much larger than they were. The best buys were made from the bus window, not only because it kept the hawkers at bay but because the prices dropped as they trotted beside the bus.

An exception to the fervid peddling was the Naguar camel fair. Traders brought camels to be raced, traded and sold at the fair. They also brought cows and horses but mostly there were camels, more camels than people. They lined the roads, the streets, vacant lots and fields. The vendors were more interested in the traders than in the tourists and set up tents to sell their wares— saddles, bridles, bells and other tack for the camels and horses, and house-hold goods for the women.

Dentists laid their instruments and whatever plates and dentures they had on a blanket at the side of the road. I stopped to take a picture of a dentist who was filing a woman's teeth. He made me promise to send him a copy of the photograph I took of him at work. Another dentist asked for $10 when I pointed a camera at him. As I walked away without a picture he said one dollar and he wanted it US. I took pictures of him pulling a woman's tooth and I gave him a dollar and a dollar to the woman. The dentist tried to take the patient's dollar but I said it was for her. I don't know what happened to the dollar after I left.

Many of those on the city and village streets chewed tobacco or betel, or had respiratory problems because of the smog. They spat in the street. There were no public toilets so men relieved themselves where they stood, usually facing a tree or a wall if one was available. The walls of the cities were streaked with urine. It ran across the sidewalks and puddled in the street. The national smell of India was urine.

To avoid dehydration it was necessary to drink a lot of bottled water but drinking a lot of water required a lot of bathroom stops. Restaurants, museums and monuments were welcome sources of public toilets. There was always an attendant. Sometimes the attendant turned on the water, sometimes he handed me a limp, wet towel, and he expected a tip. They were happy with a one rupee tip but anything below a ten rupee note was difficult to get. When I changed money, I was supposed to get 1408 rupees but the hotel had nothing smaller than a ten, meaning I got 1410 rupees. I tried to buy change from the gift shops in the hotel because my grandson collected coins but they had no coins.

I thought the attendants were intrusive and ten rupees, about twenty-five cents, too much to pay each time I took a leak although I had once paid a dollar for a toilet in Hanoi. When I learned that cleaning toilets, sweeping streets and handling the dead were jobs for the untouchables I was happy to give them a ten rupee tip.

In the countryside there were no service stations or Rest Areas. The only solution was to seek a site not too close to a house, and if possible, offering some screening by bushes or trees on one side. Bladder control improved dramatically after the first day in the country. Caffeine intake plummeted.

The highways, even major highways, were narrow, potholed and crowded. Because there were no shoulders, pedestrians and bicyclists traveled on the road. So did donkey, ox, buffalo and camel carts. There were also small, one lung tractors that looked like garden tractors that pulled large trailers filled with hay, rocks or people. Many of them served as country buses. Meeting or passing another vehicle meant both vehicles had to turn off the road. Consequently, the edges of the asphalt had been eaten away and sometimes disappeared for long stretches.

When the bus we rode met an on-coming truck both came to a stop in the middle of the road so that the drivers could slowly maneuver around each other. A driver repairing a flat had to crawl under his car so the bus could pass.

Traffic accidents were common and fatal. Ten women were killed and sixteen injured when a truck hit a minivan. The victims were riding in as well as on top of the minivan.

Most trucks and buses carried an assistant. The assistant kept his head out the window opposite the driver to be certain the bus cleared traffic, and signaled the driver to stop or move ahead by tapping on the side of the bus. He also jumped out at toll stations to pay the toll, to guide the driver when the bus had to back up, and to present papers at roadblocks on roads leading to Pakistan. Drivers were also cautioned to be careful by speed bumps at the edge of every village.

Roads and streets were also crowded with cows. I knew that cows were revered in India. I was not prepared to see them standing or lying in the middle of busy intersections, walking or sleeping on the sidewalks even in Delhi, the capital of India. There were cows everywhere. Women collected the dung, pounded it into round mounds, made a handprint so they could identify it, and stacked it to dry so it could be sold or used for fuel. Stacks of dung lined the streets, the highways, the yards, and roofs of houses. Even on the banks of the sacred Ganges.

Although cows were usually the most visible, monkeys abounded on city rooftops and sometimes injured people by throwing or toppling things into the street below. Dogs roamed freely, apparently without homes. Many of the dogs suffered mange and were bloody from scratching themselves.

Scraps of food, clothing, leftovers from living, eating, sleeping, and commerce were dumped on the street. Metal, glass, paper, and bits of good cloth were recycled or collected for reuse but there was litter everywhere, much of it scraps of plastic that would survive for years. Even the countryside was littered with plastic. The only trash bins I saw were at the airport. Sometimes women swept trash into piles with bundles of branches but I never saw any of the piles picked up. They were scattered by buses and cars and by pigs rooting through them.

Pigs ran loose on the streets. Muslims didn't eat pork and I was told that the pigs were not eaten by Hindus; the pigs kept the streets clean. The pigs, goats, dogs, and sometimes cows, foraged in trash piles and open sewers.

We walked through the narrow streets of the old city of Varanasi but were able to see little because we had to watch where we stepped. It was impossible to walk without stepping in animal feces. Cats were scarce because Indians considered them "robbers." Nevertheless, I saw no mice or rats. Maybe there was something to be said for pigs cleaning the streets. But who cleaned up after the pigs?

Although cows were revered they were also used to pull plows and carts. Buffalo, camels, and donkeys were also used. One morning on a major thoroughfare in Delhi a man riding a burro that would be small in Mexico herded seven other donkeys down the street.

Animals were not dispatched when they were old, sick or weak. They were left to struggle while crows pecked out their eyes and dogs attacked their anus until death mercifully relieved them. I thought it was cruel but Ajay said it was nature's way. Nature's way was for tigers and other predators to kill the old, sick and weak in a relatively quick and painless way. Man disrupted that way and since we had perverted nature and in some cases improved it, it seemed we should do whatever we could to relieve suffering for all living things.

I was told that the cows roaming the streets had no owners. They were no longer able to reproduce so they were turned loose. Devout Hindus fed them. Ajay explained, "India has no program for old people but there is one for old cows."

Pigeons were also fed, usually outside the mosques and temples. There were huge flights of pigeons on the ground and overhead and the birds were not denied entry into mosques and temples. We entered mosques and temples by walking barefoot over pigeon droppings while protecting our head. Feathers floated in the pool in front of the largest mosque in India. The pool was for the faithful who had to wash and brush their teeth before entering the mosque. I could only guess at what the bottom of the pool looked like.

Dead animals were not burned or buried. The carcasses were dragged to the side of the road and left to feed the animals and birds. Crows were abundant. It was nature's way, and it was the work of the untouchables to stack up the bones. Cows, plus trash, open sewers, and carcasses meant flies and even in winter they were abundant.

The people were handsome, the result of centuries of invasion by soldiers and merchants. And they were friendly. In the country-side, they stared at us with unembarrassed curiosity and usually waved. Children ran beside the bus waving, apparently wanting to be noticed. I remembered a similar feeling as a child, waving at passing trains, delighted when someone noticed that I was alive. It must be akin to writing graffiti, publishing a poem, creating or defacing a statue—compelling people to recognize your potential.

Indians treated Westerners with a deference that was troubling, probably a remnant of British occupation. Inside museums, forts, palaces, parks, Indians gave us right of way. Shop keepers bowed and invited us into their shops. Doormen snapped to attention with a salute. It was hard not to return the salute but I thought it would be condescending or mockery.

At the train station, after we fought past those who wanted to sell us something, carry our bags, or lead us to the right place, we were given sanctuary until we got off the train, collected our bags, and stepped outside into the maelstrom. On the train, Westerners and Indians were segregated and there were Western style toilets that provided a seat and Indian style toilets that did not.

In Jaipur we walked down a dark street followed by a cow, down a maze of darker, narrower alleys until we reached part of the ancient city wall. We had been invited to visit an old and distinguished family. Inside the wall was a labyrinth of rooms, up stairs, down stairs, around corners. The rooms that surrounded a large courtyard were occupied by an extended family—grandmother, three sons, their wives, children and grandchildren.

The family had been given this large and favored place because of their service to the raj. The sitting room was richly decorated with beautiful china and crystal. The smoking room was adorned with mounted tiger heads, leopard skins, photographs of wild boar hunts, ancient guns and artifacts of India. We were treated with ritual British courtesy combined with Indian modesty. Dinner was under the stars on the old city wall above the courtyard. The children entertained us by singing and dancing. For me, it was too comfortable. I could get used to being treated like that, the way CEOs are treated by politicians hoping for campaign money. I can see why the British considered India paradise.

But there was trouble in Paradise. There were frequent skirmishes on the border with Pakistan and in Kashmir which both countries claimed. In Shekhawati a young Indian walked beside me. When we passed a house with a green door he pointed at it and said, "Muslim." Sometimes other children tried to join us.

He pointed out the Muslim children, attempting to discourage me from being friendly to them.

The religious divisions are deep. Ajay said that when a Pakistani cricket or soccer team beat the Indian team, Indian Muslims celebrated. He believed that if war broke out between India and Pakistan, that Indian Muslims could not be trusted to defend their country. He also said that if a Muslim and a Hindu married they could not live in their village. They would have to move to a city where no one knew them, but he found even that doubtful.

In the holy city of Varanasi many of the palaces that lined the sacred Ganges were empty because the inhabitants had lost their wealth and power to the Muslims. Many of the temples were in disuse. When an image was broken in a temple, people no longer worshipped there and a new temple was built. Often the images were defaced by those who did not respect the Hindu religion, who believed the images were idols. There among the Hindu temples, along a river holy to the Hindus, was a mosque.

Three hundred and ten years ago Muslims destroyed a temple and built the mosque on top of the ruins. The temple priests saved the image of the sacred bull by dropping it in the well. When it was found, it was restored and a temple build around it beside the mosque.

Recently, Hindus in another city destroyed a mosque that had been built over a temple that had been destroyed to make room for the mosque. The government feared that other such mosques, like this one, would be destroyed. Barbed wire and bunkers were placed in the few feet between the temple and the mosque and national police armed with automatic weapons and wearing flak jackets stood guard between the two holy places. It was a scene out of Jerusalem where synagogues were destroyed to make churches, destroyed to make mosques, destroyed to make churches, destroyed to make mosques, destroyed to make synagogues.

The contrasts in India were startling. The English language newspaper carried a story about a hyena or panther in one district that was killing cattle. A man worshipping in a temple was killed by a tiger that escaped from the Delhi zoo. A tourist was killed in New Delhi when a monkey tipped an urn off the top of a building. Every newspaper reported people killed in the provinces during the elections. There was a protest by lawyers in Delhi that was broken up by police. A village woman was sacrificed to appease God. In some villages women had to cover their faces and were not permitted to sit in chairs but had to sit on the floor at the feet of their husband.

One evening my wife and I went to an outskirt of Delhi to have dinner with a prosperous Indian family living in a guarded community. We were welcomed into a comfortable home that could have been in a suburb in the US. It looked a little run down but that may have been because services in India were not so good, even for those who could afford carpenters, painters, plumbers. Our host was an optometrist. Before dinner we were offered hor d'ouerves and were engaged in conversation by his wife who spoke excellent English, read widely, and owned her own business.

Although vulnerable to pickpocketing in pressing crowds of hawkers I encountered no Americans who had their pockets picked. Twice I overpaid after long haggling over an item and in both instances the hawker explained my mistake and took only the amount agreed upon. Once a vendor did not have five rupee change, maybe twelve cents. I never expected to see the money but when he sold another item he found me and gave me the change.

Indian airport security was the tightest I had ever seen and I had been in Vietnam during the war, Cambodia when the Vietnamese occupied the country but the Khmer Rouge controlled the countryside, and in Northern Ireland during The Troubles. In order to fly to Nepal we had to show tickets to get into the airport terminal, stand by our checked baggage until it was x-rayed. The locks on our bags were wrapped in tape and then turned over to the airline. Our carry-on luggage was x-rayed, followed by a hand-search of the carry-ons. We walked through a metal detector, got a wand frisk, followed by a hand frisk. Then we had to go through another check to leave the terminal, walk out on the tarmac and claim our checked bags before they were loaded on the airplane. We were again frisked at the bottom of the steps to the airplane. I didn't complain about the security. Once I thought it would be an adventure to be hijacked to some remote and exotic place. That time has passed.

Upon returning to India we had to fill out the usual form. An additional section of the form had to filled out if you expected your baggage to be mishandled while in India. Maybe it was a bad translation. Beside me was a young man from Singapore. He came to India several times a year on business, moving to a different city every night. He didn't like India and wanted to return home. I said we had been to Singapore and liked the order and cleanliness. He said, "Yes, but..." And that was the end of the conversation on Singapore. In every country there is always a "but."

We rode a rickshaw to reach Delhi's crowded Chandni Chowk bazaar. The rickshaw driver had to wend his way through cars, bicycles, pedestrians, motorbikes, and flights of three-wheel taxis. At one crowded intersection, two ox carts met and there was an argument with words, gestures and pushing of each other's cows to determine the right of way.

When traffic came to a frequent stop, it crowded together and the rickshaw driver had to turn the front wheel of his bike to allow pedestrians a narrow passage. Getting started again after such a stop or pedaling out of a chughole was all in a day's work for the driver but it looked painful to me. Like most Americans I felt a vague unease at being pedaled by someone smaller than myself, affluent Westerner riding on the labor of the East. Those feelings were complicated when I learned there was a movement to outlaw rickshaws despite protests. It would put an entire industry out of business, not just the drivers but those who made and repaired the bicycles and the tires.

In a village some farmers watered down the milk. Women shoppers dipped their hands in the milk to see how quickly it ran off. Then they licked the remaining milk from their hands before testing milk from another can. A camel passed pulling a wagon of computers. A man came around the corner of a outdoor cafe buttoning his trousers, washed his hands in a bucket of water, and then poured the water into drinking glasses set on the tables.

We visited homes of professionals, merchants, farmers, and homes in some villages that scarcely deserved the name house. Eventually, we returned to our luxurious hotel that could have been in Europe or the US and bore little resemblance to the houses we had visited.

In one city we ate in a hotel that could have been any place in America—spacious lounges, gift shops, pool surrounded by young women in bikinis, a restaurant that featured roast beef, mashed potatoes, and ice cream. Outside, a barbed wire fence separated the parking lot from sacred cows and stacks of drying dung.

There were many poor in India, desperately poor, but the country was rich in history, in temples, palaces, forts, hunting resorts. The government buildings looked like government buildings everywhere—grandiose, imposing and inefficient. And like government buildings everywhere, outside the buildings were hawkers, trained monkeys, and snake charmers.

The palace forts such as Delhi's Red Fort rivaled anything in England from the same period. In the 1850's the cartridges for the new British rifles were coated with oil from cattle and swine. The end of the cartridges had to be bitten off. The Indians wouldn't put beef in their mouths and the Muslims wouldn't put pork in theirs. British officers punished those who refused to load their rifles. The Indian solders rebelled, seized Delhi, killed the Europeans and restored the former Mogul king of Delhi to the fortress palace known as the Red Fort.

"Why is it called the Red Fort?" a tourist asked.

"Because it is red and because it is a fort."

"How do you spell the first word?"

"R-E-D."

The rebellious Indian Army established Indian control of the country. The British army was sent to replace the East India Company and regain control of India. When the British army recaptured Delhi, the Red Fort was the last defense to fall. The former king was captured and his sons killed.

The immense Agra Fort was occupied for four centuries by Mogol or Mongol emperors, descendents of Genghis Khan. During the revolt of the Indian army, one British battalion held the fort and it became a refuge for Europeans from other provinces. In the courtyard was the grave of a British officer killed by rebelling Indian soldiers. By 1877, the British had regained control and Queen Victoria was declared Empress of India.

We rode elephants up the hill to the Amber Fort and palace. The fort, from the 16th century, was built on four levels and had been well preserved. The walls and ceilings of the palace were decorated and in the bedroom of the maharaj, the ceiling was covered with tiny mirrors so that in candlelight it resembled a starry night. A slave girl dancing with a candle in each hand not only showered the maharaj with love but with shooting stars.

I'd ridden elephants before so I wasn't impressed with the ride until I realized the reason for the curving entranceways, staggered barriers, and sharpened points that protruded from the gates of the fort. For centuries elephants had been used to batter in the gates of forts and it was necessary to prevent them from attacking the gates with momentum.

The Hawa Palace, called the Palace of the Winds because of the 953 windows, was not actually a palace but a facade. Women of the palace used the windows to watch the outside and forbidden world without being seen. Peeping Tomies on the sideshow that was life.

Fatehpur Sikri was a ghost city surrounded by a 117-mile-long wall, founded by Akbar the Great in the 16th century. I asked if Akbar didn't mean great and I was told it was the name of the emperor. Although the emperor was Muslim he had Hindu and Christian wives and their apartments were decorated with representational art. Representational art was forbidden in Muslim quarters because of the Biblical Second Commandment.

Orcha was once the capital of a kingdom. A large but decaying fortress and palace remained. Along the banks of the river the huge shrines to the dead rulers were visited only by cows.

Mukund Garh, a small fort, had been turned into a hotel. The walls were high, the gate narrow, the parade ground lined with flowers and the building a maze of halls, steps, rooms opening into other rooms. Finding the dining room in time for breakfast was an adventure and I bumped my head several times trying to get through the low entrance into our lodgings. We had a small sitting room and a bedroom with a bathroom reminiscent of Chillicothe, circa 1940.

There were famous havelis in Shekawati, religious frescos that became more decorative over time. We walked through the narrow streets that were crowded with goats, pigs, laughing children, working women, men sitting or lounging, talking, spitting, eating. I craned my neck to focus on the havelis under the rooftops, suffering sensory overload. There was too much to see, my eyes overwhelmed with the colors and images of the havelis, the flashing teeth of the men, the curious eyes of the children. Too much to smell, to hear, to experience. I needed time and silence to absorb but there was little time and there were tourists who had to talk away every experience, smear every sight, every taste with their comparisons to how things were done in California.

I retreated to the walls of the fort that offered several vantage spots for viewing sunset over Shekawati. Life on the street slowed, men returned to their houses. Children became quieter. Then they spotted me on the wall. "Hello, pen. Hello, pen," they cried.

We spent a lot of time getting to Khajuraho to see the Erotic Temples of the Chandelas. British archeologists excavated the temples during colonial times and the Brits were scandalized. Some of the temples were destroyed or the images defaced by moralists but eighteen temples remained. The temples were reminiscent of Angkor Wat although not so grandiose. The stone was intricately carved and rather than a repetition of figures as I

saw at Angkor Wat and the temples of Egypt, these were indi-
vidualized.

What was their purpose? I tried to find a parallel with Song
of Songs—why is it in the Bible? Because love may be illicit but it
is never profane?

One theory held that the temples demonstrated forms of love
as there seemed to be a hierarchy ranging from bestiality, to human sexuality, to the gods making love. Another theory was that
the priests wanted to encourage population growth, perhaps during one of the many invasions of India, because the carvings de-
picted what was supposed to be every possible position for the
act of love. There were some indications that Hindu worship included sexual relations with temple prostitutes. There was fur-
ther evidence of that in Nepal. The skill of the artists was
impressive but the pornography was tame by twenty-first century
internet standards.

Another monument to love was the Taj Mahal that took seventeen years and 20,000 workers to build. I had never been impressed with pictures of the Taj. It seemed too formal, too thought
out. I confess that those feelings fled when I saw it. I was impressed at its immensity and glory, stunned as it changed color
as morning broke and the sun rose. It was magnificent.

On another day we boarded a boat at Varanasi to see the sun
rise on the Ganges. Hindus worshiped the sun so sunrise was the
holiest time for bathing in the Ganges, a religious duty. There
were broad steps from the temples or ghats to the river. Monkeys
ran along the tops of the temples and palaces. Cows stood on the
steps. Cow dung was stacked along the banks. In one section,
washermen had arranged flat rocks so they could wash clothes
by dunking them in the polluted river and beating them on the
rocks. The wet clothes were then laid on the ground. Ajay said
when they dried, the washermen picked them up and shook off
the dirt.

Along the river the devout brushed their teeth, washed their
faces, waded into the water, and submerged themselves seven
times. Beside one old man who submerged himself were two

young Japanese women who had waded in up to their knees and lacked the courage to go farther. On the banks were the crematoriums where the dead were brought on bamboo ladders and burned on funeral pyres. Their relatives waited nearby then picked out the bones and threw them in the river. All the ashes would be swept into the river.

Later, far upstream in Nepal we would visit a crematorium. A steam shovel stood in the Ganges clearing a path through the ashes. Because it was dry season there was not enough water in the river to wash away the ashes that were piled so high it was necessary for the steam shovel to move them. Although the government of Nepal discouraged ceremonial bathing there because of the pollution, some devout still did so. Three pyres burned. The families stood or sat behind the pyres. The guide said it was okay to take photographs. To be sure I asked if it was disrespectful. He said no. I stood above the pyres and took a photograph of flames rising through a rib cage.

In Varanasi I washed my hands in the Ganges. I'm not sure why. I was touched by the devotion of these people, many of them poor, sick, pilgrims who had traveled for a long time. Maybe it was to show reverence to these people and their devotion. Faith in God, in whatever form it took, should be respected. However, it was difficult to understand these people with their hundreds of temples to hundreds of gods, subjecting themselves to a rigid caste system, hoping for a better life in the next reincarnation, perhaps reincarnation as a cow, while praying for enlightenment so that they were not reincarnated. "When the jewel of creation is on the lotus, let me not be reborn to this life," they prayed.

Whatever my reason for washing my hands in the Ganges, it wasn't just for the experience, like kissing the Blarney stone. The water was silty from the ashes. A dead cow floated in the water less than twenty feet away.

There was a stupa in Varanasi marking the site of Buddha's first sermon, and his monastery was being excavated. Buddha was born in Nepal but spent most of his life in India. However, there are few Buddhists in India. Most of those at the stupa were

Buddhists from other countries. Three Tibetan nuns who could speak no English signaled that they wanted to take our picture. Then we took their picture. Then we had a picture taken of all of us together. Not all pictures are worth a thousand words but this one was—Americans and Tibetans, Christians and Buddhists linked for a moment by respect for Buddha.

Another sacred place was the site where Gandhi was cremated. Gandhi did not want a huge shrine in the style of the British or Indian rulers. He wanted to be remembered as a simple man. Supposedly Ho Chi Minh wanted to be remembered the same way but neither those who built his mausoleum nor those who opposed him remember Ho that way. In contrast, the shrine erected by the government to honor Gandhi is simple and dignified. There were no soldiers standing guard, no police forcing people into conformity as at Ho's mausoleum. There were crowds of people but they were quiet, respectful, perhaps thoughtful.

My favorite place in India was Ranthambore, the tiger preserve. We stayed at an historic hunting lodge, small, rustic but with beautiful grounds. The gateway into the preserve was by a narrow chasm through the mountains. An ancient stone gate, like a block house, guarded the entrance. A dam had been built across the narrow river that had cut the chasm and water poured out of the head of a cow representing Shiva.

Beyond the gate the land opened to some of the most beautifully rugged country I have ever seen—one hundred square miles of lakes, forest, open plains, rugged mountains. Temples and ancient hunting lodges slowly decayed as banyan trees grew over, through, and around them. The country reminded me some of Big Bend; the ruined temples and lodges were reminiscent of illustrations for Gibbons' *Decline and Fall of the Roman Empire*. It reminded me most of Japanese paintings of trees growing out of craggy rocks and sheer cliffs.

We saw sambar, nilgai, chital, jackal, wildcat, monkeys, deer, crocodiles, lots of birds, flocks of wild peacocks. It was strange seeing peacocks in the wild, like seeing flocks of guinea or packs of wild dogs in Africa. It's hard to believe they're wild. But we were after the Royal Bengal tiger.

There were roads through the preserve and every guide was given a different path to take. In an open vehicle we rode along one of the roads and came upon fresh tracks, the guide said no more than thirty minutes old. We backtracked to where the sign disappeared into the grass. We waited at a water hole. We drove up and back on the road but saw no signs of tiger.

We went to a lake and observed birds and when we returned to the water hole we found another vehicle with people who had seen the tiger. We had left too soon. We waited a while and then left again passing two more vehicles that had seen the tiger at the water hole. We retraced our path at breakneck speed but the tiger had left. So had the other vehicles, returning to the lodge before the preserve was closed. The driver spoke to our guide who then took a pen and let the air out of the spare tire. At the check point the driver explained that we were late because we had a flat.

The next day we tried again, passing monkeys, deer, peacocks, and a huge, deserted fort that ran for seven kilometers along the top of a sheer cliff that rose several hundred feet above our heads. One guide said it was the biggest fort in India; another that it was the biggest fort in Rajasthan.

We stopped for a stretch and a break and shortly after we came upon a jackal, and a BBC crew filming a tiger that had disappeared. Then we saw something moving through the brush. I couldn't tell what it was, just movement. The driver drove ahead to intercept it but the tiger came up behind us. The driver backed up, signaling the BBC crew to back up also and the tiger came into a clearing and lay down close by.

For a moment we watched it in awe and then something, perhaps our excitement, aroused its curiosity and it turned its head to look at us. It was a look that caused our driver to back up farther. The tiger got up, marked its spot to warn us, walked across the road, up a low hill, and out of sight. We failed to intercepted it again but no matter; we had seen a tiger, not just a glimpse but a real sighting.

There was something refreshing, cleansing about seeing a tiger after all the cows, dogs, pigs, monkeys, camels, buffaloes, even elephants that coexisted with India's burgeoning population. The tiger was in danger of extinction but not of compliance, not of utility, not even as a benevolent god.

As we left the preserve for the last time, passing beneath the immense and deserted fortress, languar monkeys, their tails making a perfect circle over their backs, ran along the top of the fortress wall. No photograph could capture and preserve it, but my memory did.

I will remember the handsome, honest people, friendly children, the toiling women who left their signatures as hand-print on houses and on cakes of dung, and the favored women who watched the world from seclusion. I'll remember the memorial to Gandhi, the stupa where Buddha preached his first sermon, the pilgrims washing away their sins in the silted but sacred Ganges, the magnificent fortresses and glorious Taj Mahal. But I think the most lasting image I have of India is that of animals scampering along the ruined wall of an ancient and heroic past.

Still the Street Without Joy ⟶

In 1970, as a reporter for TRUE Magazine, I rode with "The Wild Bunch." They had given the name "The Wild Bunch" to themselves and had painted it on the side of their guntruck, a six-by or deuce-and-a-half. The guntruck, mounted with armor plated sides and armed with two M60 machine guns, a .50 caliber machine gun, and an M79 grenade launcher, escorted convoys of five ton trucks, tankers and SeaLand vans from Da Nang north.

There is only one road north from Da Nang, the National Highway Q. L. One, a stretch of road the French called "The Street Without Joy," made famous in Bernard Fall's book by that name. The Wild Bunch escorted truck convoys on the Street Without Joy, Da Nang to Phu Bai, Gia Le, Hue, Quang Tri, Dong Ha, and firebases along the DMZ. On trips to the firebases, The Wild Bunch was joined by other escorts, a halftrack with "The Assassins," written on the side and an armored car bearing the title, "The Copulation Culmination."

Just north of Da Nang the road passes through the mountainous Hai Van Pass that G.I. truck drivers called "the pucker factor." It is six and a half miles up to the pass, six and a half miles down and under the best conditions it took the tankers and SeaLand vans of the military convoys an hour and a half of grinding through the hairpin turns, sitting ducks for ambushes.

I met the Wild Bunch at Camp Baxter, a truck park in Da Nang. The previous day their convoy had been attacked by mortars, RPGs, and small arms fire in the Hai Vai pass and The Wild Bunch had rushed into position to take up the fire so that the unarmed trucks and tankers could continue to roll. I counted one hundred and forty hits in the armor plating on the guntruck, mostly around the .50 caliber machine gun. Five RPGs failed to explode. The Wild Bunch repulsed the enemy but their driver had been killed. A wounded driver from a damaged truck took his place.

When I met them at Camp Baxter they were sullen, even surly. They had not slept the previous night nor had they bothered to clean the blood out of the cab. The Wild Bunch had spent the night mounting a second .50 caliber machine gun on the truck. I chose to ride in the back of the truck. Not only was it armor plated, it was relatively cleaner and free of blood.

We stopped at Red Beach for a final check to be certain that all drivers were in radio contact with the guntruck and that the trucks were operating adequately for the arduous trip through the Hai Van. After the brief check the convoy rolled onto Q. L. 1 for the trip up The Street Without Joy. The mood of The Wild Bunch was not improved by the clouds that obscured the pass, denying them air cover, and a waiting ambush that, held at bay by the two .50s, never got close enough to hit anything.

There was no stopping at the summit of the pass that was guarded by ARVN bunkers, pillboxes left by the French and stone forts built to protect the south from the north years before the French arrived. Coming down from the pass, a heavily loaded cargo truck lost its brakes. The bobtails that were supposed to push overloaded and overheated trucks up to the summit and then get in front to act as brakes as the trucks came down from the pass were unable to catch the runaway truck because of civilian Vietnamese cars and buses. The truck driver risked his life running the truck into a rice paddy at the base of the mountains rather than driving the out-of-control truck through the village of Lang Co where carts, peasants and children crowded the road.

Another driver lost his brakes coming down the Hai Van and the SeaLand van overturned on the shoulder of the road, high above the rocky shore below. When we passed him the driver was lying on his back beside the road, uninjured but so shaken by his narrow escape he was unable to stand.

It was one of the most treacherous and dangerous roads in the world but also among the most beautiful. I could not ignore the beauty of the waterfalls above and the ocean crashing on the rocky shore below. I was sure that some day it would be a tourist attraction.

In 1989, I returned to Vietnam and retraced the trip from Da Nang to Hue. I was not permitted to go to Quang Tri or Khe Sahn although I believe both are open now. The land was peaceful but there were few trucks and even fewer cars in the Hai Van pass. Neat concrete houses with tile roofs covered Red Beach, where once trucks lined up for a last check before attempting the pass. The old U.S. bases were scraps of memories and metal: piles of rusting wire, crushed steel helmets, shells, casings, GI cans, airplane parts. At Phu Bai some concrete remained. Camp Eagle was barren and appeared salted. Along the highway, artillery shells with fuses removed were occasionally used for mile markers.

I thought I saw Camp Baxter. There was never much at Camp Baxter and there was even less now. Even the name Camp Baxter was gone. Back in the world most people never heard of it. Those who did have perhaps forgotten, but it was named for PFC Larry Baxter, of Pierce City, Missouri, who drove a tanker carrying 5,000 gallons of gasoline. It wasn't a glamorous job, not the kind that brought promotions or medals. It was just a job that someone had to do.

I don't know anything about Baxter. His race or religion. I don't know whether he was drafted or volunteered. I don't know how he felt about the war. Or about his country. All I know is what he did. Baxter's truck was hit by a rocket propelled grenade and set afire. Baxter could have jumped out of the blazing truck and saved his life, but that would have trapped the trucks on the road behind him. Disregarding his own safety, Baxter drove the vehicle through intense enemy fire and despite being critically wounded, drove the tanker over an embankment ensuring his own death but saving the lives of his comrades.

Baxter was posthumously awarded a Silver Star, not much of an award for one's life, but a camp was named for him. Now that too was gone, having had an even shorter life than Baxter. I don't have many heroes left. One by one they crumbled on feet of clay, and I have become too old or wise or eccentric to consider rock musicians, athletes or actors as heroes. Larry Baxter is one of my heroes and I will never forget, even though Camp Baxter is gone.

The trip to the top of the pass went quickly, impossibly fast. The Hai Van was sunny, beautiful. Freedom Hill was barren of buildings but still showed the scars of the road. This time I was able to stop at the summit, look back at the long twin concrete runways of the airbase, examine the now-useless bunkers and pillboxes that guarded the pass. I felt a disappointment I am unable to explain. I had come to relive a feeling, to locate, pin down, maybe define a moment that did not come.

I got back on the bus, distracted by another American who was excited by his new camera that permitted him to film the ancient defenses that predated the French and the sprawling city below. Suddenly, coming down from the summit, I saw an overturned SeaLand van that seemed to be in the same spot I had seen the overturned one during the war, the shaken driver lying beside it. It was almost certainly not the same one, but I was so startled I could only stare, frozen, unable to snap a shot, and had to make a return trip for a photograph.

On the trip back to Da Nang there were no clouds and a few trickling streams had replaced the waterfalls. The cheerful American talked of his new camera that permitted him to photograph the glorious craggy coast, the picturesque mountain road, the exotic people. He saw nothing, nothing, and I was filled with a rage I had not known for a long time. He knew nothing, nothing of what I knew, and he will someday be followed by thousands of tourists who will know no more than he knew. I wished for an M16 so that I could poke it into the point of his jaw just below his ear, so that for a moment he would know.

Understanding Pol Pot ⟶

Everyone you talk to in Cambodia has a story about victims of atrocities by Pol Pot's troops. Some were victims because of racial impurity. A hotel waiter is from a fishing village on the coast. His mother, who was Vietnamese, his father, and seven others in his family were killed.

Some were victims because of their connection to royalty. Dr. My Samedy, Dean of Faculty of the Medical School, General Secretary of the Kampuchea Red Cross, Chairman of the Khmer National Olympic Committee, had been physician to the queen. Several times Dr. Samedy faced death at the hand of Pol Pot, but each time he survived by healing an important person in the Pol Pot government. He had been forced to dig his own grave shortly before he was rescued by the invading Vietnamese Army.

Some were victims because they were intellectuals. Vandy Kaon, Director of the Institute of Sociology, has been described by the New York Times as "the country's leading intellectual." Pol Pot gave him a prescription written in French and asked him to read it. Vandy Kaon pretended he could not read French by trying to read it upside down, saving his life.

Some were victims because they failed Pol Pot's expectations or demands. Tuol Sleng, a high school, was turned into a torture chamber where engineers, doctors, teachers, monks, the Cambodian diplomatic corps, and Pol Pot cadre—including high ranking officers, the minister of information and vice minister of foreign affairs—were imprisoned with their wives and children. Of the 20,000 prisoners, only seven survived.

How does the world explain Pol Pot, who was more vicious than Hitler, although on a smaller scale? Pol Pot had been a high school history teacher whose students said he was very gentle and very strict. Vandy Kaon described him as a young lady who is very gentle and very cruel. One member of the present government described him as being an excellent speaker, "with the voice of an angel and the heart of a devil."

"Shadows of Darkness," one of three films produced by the Institute of Sociology, is the first Khmer film about Pol Pot, and although it shows his excesses, it does little to explain what motivates such a man or what motivates others to follow him. All those involved in the film, including the actors, lived through the Pol Pot regime. They are living witnesses who fear the younger generation may forget the terror of Pol Pot.

The film is also intended to prevent the world from forgetting, or ignoring, the horror that has happened to Cambodia. Huy Sophann, producer, ruefully admitted the mixture of Rambo violence and traditional Khmer theater was an attempt to attract interest in the United States where the film has been shown. "In the West such things are necessary," he said. But no special-effects violence can suggest the real horror of what happened.

Huy Sophann, in attempting to explain the genocide of the Pol Pot regime, said there were three types of socialism: vengeful, utopian, and realistic. The Khmer Rouge was the most striking example of vengeance socialism—one social group seeking revenge on the others, particularly intellectuals, feudalists, and royalty. The Khmer Rouge did not want to build a socialist society but to seek revenge against the country and saw no difference between killing a friend and killing an enemy.

Some tried to explain Pol Pot as doctrinaire, a puritanical kind of maniacal genius, and excused Pol Pot as mentally ill. Others ascribed his atrocities to communist ideology and the influence of Maoism. According to them, every human being is an instrument for every situation. Pol Pot did not plan cruelty but became cruel to protect his regime. When his cadre failed to carry out his purposes, Pol Pot became angry and suspicious. The ultimate means of protecting his regime was terror.

Vandy Kaon believes you cannot understand Pol Pot or Cambodia without understanding the ancient Angkor empire. As a history teacher Pol Pot knew the glory of the Khmer kingdom that built Angkor Wat and Angkor Thom, a kingdom that included large portions of Laos, Vietnam and Thailand, including the cities of Vientiane, Bangkok and Saigon.

Pol Pot wanted to regain Khmer glory and to restore the country to a power greater than that of Vietnam and Thailand, to build something better than Angkor. "If our people can make the temples of Angkor, they can make anything," he said. He believed that Cambodia had lost its glory and become weak because of the laziness of the people, middle class decadence, and a change from Brahminism to Buddhism, a religion that taught patience and that progress did not come about through desire but through enlightenment. Only Marxism could make the country prosperous and powerful, and only a primitive, agrarian form of Marxism.

Pol Pot was the ultimate fundamentalist. The way to the future was through dismantling the decadence of the present until one had returned to the glories of Angkor. Such a message had the appeal of Jimmy Swaggart, Tammy Faye, even Ron and Nancy. The Khmer people supported Pol Pot until they saw his excesses.

Because Buddhism had caused the downfall of Cambodia, Pol Pot tried to destroy the Buddhas and pagodas, and made the monks pull plows like oxen.

Because the people were lazy and non-productive he drove them from the cities into slave camps in the country where they were to be cleansed by hard work from the taint of foreign ideas and middle class values. Many died under the harsh conditions or were killed because they were too weak to work and therefore of no value to the revolution. "To have them is no gain, to lose them is no loss," their masters said.

Every brick of the cathedral was taken away because it represented prosperity. The best homes in every village were destroyed because they were symbols of the last regime. Pol Pot tried to destroy good things from the past so that the young would not know the past, only socialism.

Because he feared foreign ideas would be a fifth column, he destroyed books and schools and killed teachers, students, ethnic Vietnamese, and anyone who could speak a foreign language.

Because of the past expansionist nature of Vietnam and because he believed that Vietnam was scheming to conquer Cambodia, he declared, "We must not only stop them and annihilate them in our territory, but must cross the border to stop them and annihilate them right on their territory." Pol Pot ordered border raids on Vietnam and Thailand and made plans to "recapture" Saigon.

When his army recoiled at a Vietnamese counter-raid, Pol Pot began killing the officers, including division commanders, because of their weakness. This provoked a brief civil war and captured rebel troops, their families, and villages that sheltered them were slaughtered.

The "killing fields" of Cambodia were not the irrational act of a madman, or an accident. Pol Pot was one of those intelligent men who intend to make the world perfect, or at least nearly so, no matter what the cost. "It took lot of planning to do what he did," Vandy Kaon said. The failure of those plans drove Pol Pot to even greater excesses.

Is there any way the world can protect itself against such zealotry? Perhaps not. Such men will always find a following among romantics who dream of a return to Eden or Angkor, fanatics who believe in the perfectibility of humanity and its institutions, and opportunists who glean success from the spillage of excess.

If there is a lesson to be learned, it is perhaps that no nationality is inherently superior to another. "In terms of numbers, one of us must kill thirty Vietnamese," said Pol Pot, echoing words heard before the Alamo and after Pearl Harbor. The past has many lessons to teach us but the way to the future is not by recreating the past, and the way to Eden is not by the wholesale destruction of the structures and institutions of the present. Progress may be so slow as to be indiscernible, but every great leap forward has been a bloodstain on the record of human achievement.

Pol Pot's Legacy ~

1989

Most of the world knows that the genocidal Pol Pot killed an estimated two or three million Cambodians, approximately one-third of his countrymen. That horror has loomed so large that a lesser crime has been overlooked—Pol Pot's devastation of his country. Pol Pot left behind him a populace threatened with famine in a country in which he had abolished money, markets, schools, hospitals and the postal system, in which the infrastructure of clerks, electricians, plumbers, engineers and mechanics had either fled or been killed. This has caused enormous problems for the Vietnamese-installed Phnom Penh government. Almost all those problems will remain for whatever government is selected whenever peace comes.

Phnom Penh is both a symbol and an example of what has happened to the country. After heavy shelling of Phnom Penh, Pol Pot's army captured and looted it. The inhabitants were driven out of the city and for three years and eight months Phnom Penh was deserted. Then the Vietnamese captured the city and systematically plundered it.

As the fighting moved into the countryside, frightened villagers sought refuge in the ravaged city bringing their tribal ways with them. They moved into whatever building was available, tying their pigs and chickens to streetlamps or keeping them on the balconies of villas or office buildings. They broke into the city's water mains to use for village wells, cooked on fires built on floors or sidewalks and threw their garbage into the street.

Brett Ballard, who is working with American Friends Service Committee, said, "What you have is a city being run by farmers who don't know cars, electricity, sewage, water systems, transportation or communication."

In Phnom Penh everything is jury-rigged. Rows of car batteries line a hotel lobby to operate lobby lights when the electricity fails, as it does several times a day. Naked wires run from upper stories of buildings and tie into power lines in the street. Room fans are operated by taking wires and poking the exposed ends into holes in the wall until a connection is made. In every hotel bathroom there is a large pail. Whenever there is water, the hotel guests fill the pail and use it for bathing, shaving, and flushing the toilet.

Outside the hotel is the beginning of a beggar class, the young and the old. Children make play teapots from the mud of the gutter. Work parties are conscripted for public work and children with brooms and hoes are paraded through the streets to cut grass and clean up rubbish.

More serious problems are less visible. Uch Kiman, Director, General Policy Department, Ministry of Foreign Affairs, is an archaeologist pressed into service as a diplomat. When he returned to Phnom Penh after the Vietnamese had "liberated" the city, he found rare and priceless books from the National Library scattered in the street. Between 60 and 70% of the library's books had been destroyed.

The Library and the National Museum were used to house and raise animals. The cathedral was torn down and the bricks carried away so that nothing remained. The best houses were destroyed because they represented the prosperity of the colonial regime. The only reason the National Palace was not destroyed was because China, Pol Pot's only ally, asked him to take care of Prince Sihanouk.

Pol Pot destroyed archaeological research including many monuments and antiquities. The Phnom Penh government has appealed to citizens to preserve antiquities and to collect them and is trying to educate the young to the glories of Cambodia's past.

Uch Kiman became emotional as he described the many things that he had once studied and admired that had been destroyed. The government lacks the money to collect and preserve all the antiquities and restore the monuments so they must decide priorities, but few archaeologists survived the Pol Pot regime.

The National Theater still stands but shows signs of neglect. Traditional dancers were killed or fled the country. An older dancer was used to teach orphans nine years old and younger in order to resurrect traditional dances. It takes ten years to train a traditional dancer and beginners must be no older than nine in order to have the flexibility for the beautiful but unnatural hand movements.

Vandy Kaom, Director, Institute of Sociology, pointed out another problem. Because of insecurity in the countryside, refugees crowd into Phnom Penh. The government tries to arrange cinemas and to guarantee schools and medical care in the villages to attract them to return, but it is difficult because of security reasons. The government gives special praise to teachers who work in the provinces because the Khmer Rouge has tried to terrorize them. As an incentive to encourage doctors to work in the provinces the government offers to upgrade their training.

Pol Pot had collectized the farms but the Phnom Penh government has restored private property and given the land to the farmers to encourage them to return to the villages. To counter the mass unemployment in the city the socialist government has permitted private enterprise in order to create jobs. In an open market in Phnom Penh long rows of women sat at treadle sewing machines making jeans that had Levis labels. On the outskirts of the city is what a Thai reporter called the world's largest secondhand motorbike market where some 8,000 motorbikes are sold each day, many of them to Vietnamese who prefer the 70's model because it reminds them of the good old days.

Vandy Kaom fears that private enterprise has led to markets full of goods, poor people with no money to buy, and class divisions. Chheang Yanara, Chief of the Department of General Planning, said he was not worried about people who were better off; he was worried about people who were starving. He was echoing Prime Minister Hun Sen who was quoted in the New York Times as saying, "We are not looking to building up Marxism or Communism. We are looking to improve the welfare of the people."

The government has averted famine and now is trying to recover industry that had been destroyed by Pol Pot. The state remains in charge of major industry. Chheang Yanara believed it would be easier to restore the economy when there was a political settlement of the civil war. One hopeful sign was that Thai industry lacks timber and Cambodia has an abundance of timber but lacks hard currency.

The country is in desperate need of hard currency to buy spare parts for tools and machinery. There is more electrical power than before but they have not been able to meet the present need. Pol Pot and the war have destroyed many roads. The government is rebuilding the roads but has to reduce its balance of payment to do so. And the country needs more students, teachers and medical workers.

My Samedy, M.D., Dean of Faculty of Medical school, said that only forty-five doctors survived the Pol Pot regime. Fifteen of those left the country. Only 128 medical students survived out of approximately 300. Textbooks and labs were destroyed along with the chairs from the amphitheater. Refrigerators were overturned and surgical equipment torn apart. The library is kept in one room; most American high schools have more books. Papers and other trash litter the halls and corners of the classrooms.

Dr. Samedy enumerated the country's medical problems. Pol Pot didn't understand the sewer system was connected to the Mekong River and that during high water the exit pipes had to be blocked. Silt filled the sewer system which broke into the water system. The water is not safe to drink. Residents of the city are troubled with dysentery and typhoid. The city has no garbage trucks, no equipment, and no way to dispose of garbage.

Phnom Penh did not have malaria before Pol Pot sent the residents to the forests. Now one third of the population has malaria and 100 people die of malaria every day. No one knows if there is AIDS in Cambodia because they don't have the equipment for testing.

Buildings collapse because they were not maintained. Recently a house near the hospital collapsed and killed eight people. The government tries to prohibit habitation in unsafe buildings but has been unable to keep people from moving in.

There have been some successes. Ninety-eight percent of the children have been inoculated for polio, measles, whooping cough, typhoid, tetanus, and diphtheria. Many folk healers were killed and traditional remedies lost. The government has encouraged the planting of herbs, has trained 400 traditional herbalists, and has recorded remedies in informational booklets.

The country has been depopulated by mass killing and mass exodus, and although some want to enlarge the population for protection against larger cultures, the government is encouraging family planning to repopulate the country without huge families.

In addition to being dean of the medical school, Dr. Samedy is responsible for resettlement of the 300,000 Cambodian refugees on the Thai border. Some want to return but not to their native village for fear of Pol Pot. Those who return to the land must have the means to rebuild homes and plant crops. Many young people have been reared in refugee camps and have never farmed. The government will prepare them for other work. The government will find work for former bureaucrats in the villages, but not in Phnom Penh.

Dr. Samedy hopes that Cambodian people who have learned trades and professions will return and help train the populace. He believes if there is a peaceful settlement the older people will come back home. What will happen if they return and someone is living in their house? So far there has been no problem. The returnees had money and paid the squatters for taking care of their homes.

Suong Saarvn, Dean of Faculty of Philosophy, University of Phnom Penh, said that out of one thousand students only ninety-three survived the Pol Pot regime. Desks, chairs, and blackboards were destroyed. Pol Pot used the university buildings for a prison and the campus had turned into a forest.

Before Pol Pot all teaching was done in French. After Pol Pot there were no teachers. For three years the university used Vietnamese professors who spoke French. This caused many problems but they had no choice. After three years they had teachers who could teach in the native Khmer language. Now all subjects are taught in Khmer.

They had to develop a technical language in Khmer and still must improve it. They also must improve their training and prepare for post graduate training. Presently there are forty students in post-graduate training but there is no professor to help them. The government needs Russian language translators, but the students don't want to learn Russian and Vietnamese. They want to learn French and English, but the university can't get enough French and English teachers. Presently they have eighty Vietnamese teachers, thirteen Russian, two French, two German, one Cuban, and two English teachers, one from Australia and one from Canada. One of the English professors was excited because the university was letting students check out books from the library. So many books had been destroyed that the remaining ones were kept under lock and key.

Mom Chim Huy, Vice Minister of Education, said that before the Vietnamese "liberation" Cambodia had over a million illiterate. The government set up a national committee to address the problem, and presently nearly 100% of urban children go to school. The percentage is smaller in rural areas, and only 50 to 60% among ethnic people in the mountains who have no written language and must be educated in Khmer.

The present goal is for all students to complete five years of schooling. Those who complete five years stay in school. The eventual goal is eight years of schooling. Some older people are forgetting their skills and are reluctant to return to studies. The remaining illiterate are nervous about learning, so the government is going to put the young illiterates and the elderly who need additional training in classes together.

The government is working hard to build schools. Pol Pot destroyed Buddist pagodas and made the monks pull plows, and the Vietnamese suppressed the religion, but the Buddhists are back in favor now and the pagodas collect money for schools. The vice minister said the people could build the buildings themselves, but the country needed help with laboratories, teacher training and publishing books. The libraries are for university students. The other schools have bookcases if they have the means.

The state gives permission for private schools in special subjects and vocational training. The most popular subject in private schools is Streamline English and the place where it is taught is called English Street. Students line up outside the buildings to pay seventy riels (about fifty cents) for two hours of classes. A new tourist hotel is being built on the bank of the Mekong and there is a rumor that only English speakers will be hired. The teachers read and write English very well but have difficulty with pronunciation because they have no English speaking models.

Only the state provides general studies to prepare students for society and the work place. The vice minister explained that this is done by teaching students moral laws, and giving them an international conscience. Giving an international conscience is teaching good traditions and world culture because the UNESCO constitution says that war comes from the hearts of men. Pol Pot taught children not to respect their parents. People were looked down on by children who became savage killers.

What happened to those children who are the real legacy of Pol Pot? Were they still fighting in the mountains? Were they obsessed with guilt? With cruelty? After they had learned such viciousness and experienced such horror could they be integrated back into society? The vice minister acknowledged this was an important problem for the government to solve.

John Wayne Must Die ⟶

When I was young, I saw a lot of John Wayne. I watched him kill a lot of people. All of them bad, most of them Indians. He was also pretty good at killing Japanese, but not so good at killing Germans. John Wayne didn't die. Heroes never die. Not in the movies.

When I was in Marine boot camp they showed us John Wayne movies. In Marine boot camp you couldn't leave the base, you couldn't go to the PX, you couldn't buy soft drinks, ice cream or candy. You couldn't have cigarettes, beer, or women. Instead, we had John Wayne. Usually, he wore a Marine uniform and killed a lot of Japanese.

An eighteen-year-old Marine boot is one of the dumbest things on earth. We didn't think catsup was a vegetable; catsup was an hors d'oeuvre. As a eighteen-year-old boot I didn't understand why we had to use the atomic bomb when we had John Wayne. He could kill as many Japanese as anyone could enjoy seeing die. And he didn't cost much more than the research and development of the atomic bomb. Not if you threw in the research and development of the B-29.

And John Wayne didn't die.

John Wayne didn't do much in Korea. Killing Indians paid better. And John Wayne didn't die.

After Korea, John and I went our separate ways. I was busy going to school, getting married, starting a career. I didn't have time for movies. I didn't see "The Alamo." I don't know how he got out of that one.

John Wayne had his own problems in Vietnam. He killed a lot of Viet Cong but no one enjoyed it. At the drive-in a few people cheered, but they were blowing grass and thought he was killing

Indians. The Viet Cong had a Benevolent and Protective Society in Berkeley and other schools of thought. The Japanese didn't have a Benevolent and Protective Society but they had Toyotas. And yen. So John went back to killing Indians. Nobody cared about Indians.

John Wayne didn't die.

John also killed some bad men. They were so bad that watching them curl up and croak was almost as pleasurable as watching the Japanese fry or seeing gut-shot Indians run over by their own horses before being scalped by Christians. Bad men weren't massacred. They died one by one, like men. There was a Benevolent and Protective Society for bad men.

John Wayne didn't kill women. No need to. Some things were lower than Indians. John Wayne didn't marry them either. He wasn't afraid of bad women, although good women gave him a scare or two. Nothing scarier than a good woman when she was breathy and in heat. John Wayne put women in their place. A little higher than a coyote. A little lower than a dead horse.

But John Wayne didn't die.

John Wayne became the hero of America, replacing such impostors as Lindbergh, Clarence Darrow, Albert Einstein, Audie Murphy, William Faulkner. He became the icon of the west, replacing such impostors as Sam Houston, Chief Joseph, Teddy Roosevelt, Bill Haywood, Will Rogers.

John Wayne was spit and image of the American hero. He was tougher than a longhorn steak until real bullets flew. He was meaner than a side-winder if someone sat on his hat, beat his woman or was discourteous to a horse. But only on film.

John Wayne was charmingly inarticulate. He had only twelve words in his vocabulary other than Winchester, six-shooter, kill, shoot, maim, horse, dog and pilgrim. Six of the remaining words were conjugations of "Wal." Don Quixote may have been addled but he wasn't incoherent. In the theater, even heroes have to speak. In novels, even stupid men have to be able to think. It took movies to give us "yep" heroes. Movies started out silent. They remained dumb; they just added sound.

John Wayne didn't need nobody. He didn't ask favors. He didn't take handouts. He pulled himself up by his own six-shooters.

John Wayne had no self-doubts. His opinion was right and you were welcome to your own as long as it agreed with his. He was on the right road, headed in the right direction and if you didn't get out of his way he'd kill you. Or maybe just maim you if you had made an honest mistake. He sometimes let women and children live. And he didn't die.

John Wayne never broke a sweat for daily bread, toiled at a repetitive and humbling job for minimum wage, or was gainfully employed, except at killing people. His only skill was violence, but it was the skill most honored and most envied by his countrymen. And he didn't die.

John Wayne loved freedom. The freedom to go wherever he wanted to go, do whatever he wanted to do, and kill anyone who wanted the same. He was the quickest to violence. Always. Leaving slower men dead in the street.

Wayne had values. Good horses. Good dogs. Good whiskey. Good violence. He hated bad violence and killed bad-violent men. He was more violent than anyone, but he killed only those he thought needed killing. He had a code that permitted no extenuating circumstances and no exceptions. Except himself.

John Wayne was innocent. No matter how many people he killed, or how much pleasure or satisfaction he got out of it, he maintained innocence about the whole bloody business. Wal, sure, some good men died too. And some women were caught in the crossfire. And some babies. Some babies always die. But when you look up there and see old glory waving in the breeze, high up there, on top of the Savings and Loan Building, it makes you wish the taxpayers weren't so gol darned cheap and had given you a few more bullets to waste. Someone with.

John Wayne didn't lose. Right means might so John Wayne couldn't lose. John Wayne wasn't at Wake Island or Corregidor because John Wayne didn't lose. He left Vietnam early.

I didn't see "The Alamo." I don't know how he got out of that. Travis died. Crockett and Bowie died. John Wayne didn't die. I've been to the Alamo. I know that John Wayne is in there somewhere. And he's alive.

John Wayne didn't die. His spirit transcended him, passed into the souls of Americans everywhere. The story that St. John bodily ascended into heaven is probably not true. John Wayne passed into the spirit of Americans who died in Beirut, Grenada, Nicaragua, Libya, Panama, Iran, Iraq. John Wayne didn't die.

John gave us the stories that tell us how to be men when women and children don't measure up to our standards for them. When other men don't get out of the way of our ambitions. When teachers, parents or peers try to fence in our egos. When inferiors pretend they have the same rights we have.

St. John taught us, big and powerful is good. Small and weak is bad and must be killed. Or at least, exploited.

St. John taught us that a man should take everything he can get, and the quickest way to get it is with a gun.

St. John taught us that the fastest to the trigger is the hero.

John Wayne lives in the souls of those who believe bullets speak louder than words, who believe a gun, a quick draw and a steady aim are the only Bill of Rights you'll ever need.

John Wayne must die.